A Prai

MW01287248

"A Prairie Almanac is a wonderful recollection of pioneer life from one who knew first hand what it was to carve out an existence on the beautiful Iowa prairies. The audience for this book is much broader than Linn County; much of the material is representative of pioneer experience throughout eastern Iowa and most of the rest of the state. Sections could be abstracted for use in the schools throughout the Midwest."—Lynn Nielsen, Ph.D., Elementary Principal, Department of Teaching, University of Northern Iowa, Cedar Falls.

"Clearly Isaac Kramer was interested in how the world around him was changing. His *Almanac* offers a look at the fun and adventure of pioneer times, and insight into how the lives we lead today evolved from those times. He could be a pioneer role model for the young."—Phyllis Fleming, The Gazette, Cedar Rapids.

"What a wonderful way to celebrate Iowa's 150th birthday, with an easy-to-read book that is historically accurate and tells it the way it was. The *Almanac* brings to life the pioneering spirit, as well as the sense of humor and intelligence required of families who made Linn County grow and become what it is today."—Onalee Paul Arnold, genealogist, Marion.

"The Almanac has the specific detail that we need when we put together a living history interpretation, and I find that Isaac Kramer writes with a good memory of specifics. Your editorial inserts supply necessary details that smooth the story line rather than distract from it."—Tom Morain, Ph.D., Living History Farms, Urbandale, Iowa.

"Jean Strong did a fine job of editing a rough manuscript. The text represents a faithful picture of early life in Iowa, with all its hardships and simpler pleasures. I enjoyed reading Isaac Kramer's *Almanac*."—Holly Carver, University of Iowa Press, Iowa City.

"It has always been important for students to make the connection between American history and Iowa's importance in it. To have detailed, first hand information about our own territory was especially appealing. Hardly a lesson went by when we were not doing comparison or reference checking; the *Almanac* proved to be a focal point in our American history classes."—Ruth Hatcher, 8th grade teacher, Prairie Junior High, College Community Schools, Cedar Rapids.

"Trivia of the past intrigues fifth graders who delight in learning about the personal experiences of Isaac Kramer—stories that cannot be found in textbooks. 'Blab' schools, sharing a hard biscuit cut with an axe, wolves digging up fresh graves on the prairie, and stories of thieves and outlaws certainly captivate the attention of the classroom. This is an excellent primary source with innumerable applications."—Susan C. Hightshoe, 5th grade teacher, Linn-Mar Intermediate, Linn-Mar Community Schools, Marion.

Celebrating the

Iowa Sesquicentennial

150 Years of Statehood

~ 1 8 4 6 - 1 9 9 6 ~

A Prairie Almanac
1839 to 1919

*The eyewitness story about
everyday life of pioneers*
as told by Isaac N. Kramer

~ Illustrated ~

JEAN STRONG

Prairie Almanac Publisher
P.O. Box 1312
Bentonville, AR 72712-1312

CREDITS and COPYRIGHTS

Permissions

Pioneer drawings by Edward J. Lettermann, courtesy of Living History Farms, Urbandale, Iowa.
Excerpt p. 39. Reprinted with permission of the State Historical Society of Iowa from Earl D. Ross, *Iowa Agriculture: An Historical Survey*, 1951.
Quotes p. 84. Reprinted with permission, from Frederick A. Norwood, *The Story of Methodism*, 1974, Abingdon Press, Nashville, Tennessee.

Illustration credits

Engravings of George Greene, p. 16, and Cornell College, p. 86, from 1911 History of Linn County, Iowa, Vols. I and II
Maps, Jean Strong, pp. 5, 8, 28, 91
Pioneer drawings throughout. Isaac Kramer frontispiece (top left), and pp. 9-125, Living History Farms, Urbandale, Iowa

Photographs

Nelda Y. Hoover Collection, Cedar Rapids: Isaac Kramer frontispiece, and pp. 15, 111, 119, 120, 121

Robert Hutton Collection, Marion: pp. 29, 35

Marion Carnegie Library, Marvin Oxley *History of Marion*, Vol. I: pp. 107 (bottom), 115, 122

Frank and Elizabeth Lund, Florida: p. 119

State Historical Society of Iowa, Iowa City: p. 107 (top)

Vivian Rinaberger Collection, Cedar Rapids: p. 124

A PRAIRIE ALMANAC 1839 to 1919,
the eyewitness story about everyday life of pioneers
as told by Isaac N. Kramer

Dedicated to our ancestors

and to those who follow

Such as my great-nieces and great-nephews

Leslie
Kathy
April
Joey
Sue Lynn
Brandon
Steven
Amber
Kim
Duncan
Heather
Holly

and Isaac's great-great-great-grandchildren

About the Editor of *A Prairie Almanac*

To Howard Powers, fellow author and old friend, with best wishes.

Jean Strong

Jean Strong grew up in Linn County, Iowa, graduated from a one-room country school, attended Marion and Springville high schools, received a B.A. degree from the University of Iowa in 1951 (journalism major with a heavy dose of political science).

Her journalistic and publishing career began in Iowa on weekly newspapers (at Marion and Center Point), and with the daily *Cedar Rapids Gazette*. She went to New York as a reporter for *Life* and *Fortune* magazines, to Philadelphia as a *Farm Journal* books editor, to Washington, D.C. and Capitol Hill.

Retired from Time-Life Books in 1986, she lives in the beautiful Ozarks of northwest Arkansas, and is writing about her life in Iowa and elsewhere. She labored lovingly for four years of the past ten readying this book for publication, and also enjoys reading, travel, and the great outdoors. Isaac Kramer is her great-great-granduncle.

CONTENTS

Eyewitness to pioneer history
ISAAC N. KRAMER
1832 - 1923

Gardener: 1840s

Nurseryman: 1860s

Author: 1900s

Introduction

ISAAC N. KRAMER was seven years old when he traveled west to Iowa. He was eighty-seven when he completed his book manuscript. This book is based on observations, thoughts, and notes made during his long life. He was a pioneer farm boy with a love for gardening. After building Linn County's first greenhouse, he became a successful seedsman and florist. Although his formal education was scant, he never lost his appetite for learning. Isaac concerned himself throughout his life with looking, listening, and learning how things work.

Isaac Kramer did not dwell on his own personal life. Those details are inserted where appropriate to put his life in context with the story he tells. Isaac describes how he and his parents journeyed from Pennsylvania on riverboats in 1839. Rich farmland in the western territory beckoned; the government promised to sell it for $1.25 an acre. Pioneers soon learned that the cost to hire someone to break prairie was twice as much as the land. Even so, many pioneers persevered. The Kramers lived out their lives in Iowa while some early settlers were enticed to seek their fortunes elsewhere —most often in areas no less challenging.

Isaac's descriptions are extraordinary in detail. He tells about everyday life as he, his family, and other pioneers lived it. He tells how log cabins and rail fences were constructed; how grain was planted, harvested, and marketed; how clothing was made with homespun material. He tells about several white men who were not good neighbors, and about some who were. He relates how his fellow scholars stopped Christmas from being observed as a school day. He does not neglect the lighter side. He describes the impact of a meteorite, and social occasions that brighten pioneer life. He compares the three organized religions that served the spiritual needs of these hardy pioneers.

Kramer had written forty-four chapters, mostly about the early days, by 1919. His story is about the evolution of society —from pioneer to post-pioneer farming. We are indebted to the State Historical Society in Iowa City, and to its superintendent in the 1920s, for preserving Isaac's 178-page typescript. It was titled "The Early Settlement of Linn County." Its present title, *A Prairie Almanac: 1839 to 1919*, better describes the content.

The Kramer manuscript lay unedited in the archives for more than sixty years. I happened upon it while searching for information about early Linn County at the time my ancestor, Luman Strong, had known it. Few people took time then to write in detail about their frontier experiences. I was surprised and delighted to find that Isaac Kramer is my great-great-granduncle, and had bothered to record his thoughts and memories. I researched and edited his manuscript, rearranged chapters, and preserved Isaac's words where possible. The words of the editor and others appear in *italics* and extend the story line.

Getting acquainted with "Uncle Isaac" has been a pleasure; making this work available in readable form is a joy.

Iowa is only one of a dozen states that nurtured the tall-grass prairies in the 1800s. This prairie stretched west from Indiana across Illinois and all of Iowa, into Nebraska, and spilled northward into the Dakotas, Minnesota, and Wisconsin. To the south, tall-grass prairie extended into Kansas, Missouri, across Oklahoma, into Texas. Splotches of tall grass dotted small areas of Ohio, Kentucky, Arkansas and Louisiana—but Iowa was the heart of the prairie. Many conditions and experiences Isaac describes were shared by thousands of the earliest settlers.

Jean Strong
Bella Vista, Arkansas
June 15, 1996

1 Isaac in Pennsylvania

MY early home in a little village in Pennsylvania boasted a glass factory and a foundry. It was a rough place for bringing up boys, but I did not live there long enough to be seriously influenced by associations of the place. I have no distinct memory of incidents in my life before entering school at age five. I was sent to a 'loud school' so that I might learn to talk. I had depended on motions and inarticulate sounds to express my wants.

Probably Isaac's wishes and wants were anticipated by his older brother and other siblings, making talk unnecessary. Isaac was the tenth child of Andrew Kramer. In those early days, children were encouraged to be seen and not heard. At loud school, all students read their lessons out loud at the same time. Some schools in the 1800s were called 'blab' school.

As the name indicates, the school was a noisy one. Children vied with one another to see who could make the loudest noise. If the intention was for us all to repeat the lesson in unison, that idea was not impressed upon my budding mind. I remember only the louder and more irregular sounds. How that technique affected my learning to talk I cannot say. I think I soon engaged in the universal jabber. Part of my trouble was fearing to speak lest I should fail to say my words properly and be laughed at or scolded.

The great financial crisis of 1837 occurred about the time I first attended school. All business came to a standstill. Businessmen with debts were ruined; my father among them. Property was impossible to sell, and wages were reduced to a pittance. As a practical matter, no employment for labor existed. Men so completely thrown out of business were compelled to seek a way for making a living from the soil. Consequently, over the next few years a great exodus took place to new and unsettled parts of the country. Men sought claims where they could build cabins, and occupy the land until the opportunity for buying it occurred.

My 48-year-old father was completely broken up. He soon sought a new home—away from the glass factory he and others had organized. He went to Iowa for a visit in the summer of 1838. The first person he met on Iowa soil was a man who had been an employee at the glass factory; Jimmy Beaty took Father to his home about 10 miles away. From there Father went on foot to Linn County. It was about a 50-mile walk. He found a number of persons mostly at Westport and Ivanhoe—*towns that had been staked out in the county that very year.*

Father located a claim in the eastern part of the county; the area would be known as Linn Grove. On his return trip he stopped in Ohio and asked his oldest son, Lewis, to precede us next summer. Lewis would take his family and team, build a cabin, and occupy the claim. *Lewis is Isaac's oldest half-brother.*

2 River Route to Iowa

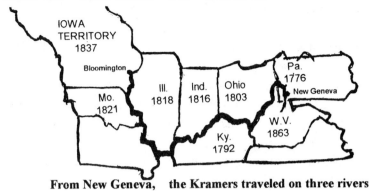

From New Geneva, the Kramers traveled on three rivers

FATHER started for Iowa the following September, traveling with his wife and six children in a keelboat named *Star*. This boat was comparatively long and narrow. Its low freight deck, although covered, was not high enough for a person to stand in upright. Its steering oar had a paddle on the end and was attached to the stern (rear) of the boat. An iron bolt served as a pivot. The paddle could be raised from or lowered into the water as needed. The helmsman stood or sat where he could watch both fore and aft and guide the boat. Pike poles pushed the boat along when it could not be floated, or had to go upstream. These poles had steel points that could be thrust into the riverbed. A cross piece on the upper end afforded a pushing point to make the boat move forward. A runway on either side of the boat deck was outfitted with naileddown cross pieces for bracing the feet while pushing. Oarsmen stepped from brace to brace until they got to the afterdeck. Then each went back with his pole and repeated the process.

The Monongahela flowed northward in the direction of our travel from our old home in New Geneva. About 30 miles north, Father stopped to take on board his son-in-law and family. *The Andrew Kramer travel party now includes Andrew and wife, seven children, a son-in-law, and one grandchild. Andrew has married three times; his first two wives died. Four children from the second marriage making the trip are: Christeen 24, Andrew L. 15, Mary Elizabeth 13, and Ann 21 with her hus-*

band, *Barnet Lutz, and their child. Three children from Andrew's third and current marriage are also on this boat: Michael 9, Isaac 7, Amy 16 months. Mrs. Kramer and Mrs. Lutz are both in circumstances (expecting babies).*

At Pittsburgh the Kramer keelboat entered the Ohio river and began its float past Ohio, Indiana, and Illinois to their right, and West Virginia and Kentucky on their left. The Ohio river forms boundaries for those five states. Keelboats in the early 1800s transported flour, whiskey, iron, and glass, with merchandise and immigrants bound for Kentucky and Ohio.

On the Ohio we met with many dangers between Pittsburgh and Cincinnati. These included snags, hidden rocks, and dams to jump. The steamboat *Albert Gallatin* came near to sinking us with its high waves. This boat was familiar to me. It had been built at New Geneva in 1839 under the direction of my first school teacher, Freeman Smith. With other small boys, I had watched day-to-day progress until the boat was launched. When it passed us, it was probably on its way to the lower Mississippi. *Two years later, in January 1842, the steamer blew up in the Gulf of Mexico between Galveston, Texas and New Orleans, killing five and wounding nine passengers and crew* (Lloyd, p. 288).

Later on, a nearly grown boy hailed the *Star* and asked if he might work his passage down river. Father agreed—if he was a good hand. "I am all that and more, too," he said. The boat was run to shore and he came on board. Although quite reckless, the fellow proved to be an excellent hand. He knew the river thoroughly from previous trips. His story was that he had run away from home. His Methodist minister father often entertained fellow ministers, he said. On this occasion when the lad saw one coming, he ran to the chicken coop and created turmoil among the chickens. His father reproved him severely. The boy maintained the coming of the minister had caused the fuss, that he was trying only to quiet the chickens. The boy had hailed our boat after his father whipped him.

Father decided to abandon the *Star*, leaving it for sale at Cincinnati. He took passage on a steamer for the two families to continue. However, our progress was little better than we had made on the keelboat. The river was so low that hardly a day passed when we were not stuck fast on some sandbar. We spent two or three days on the Cumberland bar. To relieve our hunger, our parents obtained a little flour that produced some of the best bread I ever ate. Mother mixed the flour with river water and baked it on coals. We finally succeeded in getting the boat off the bar after the men lightened it by unloading the goods and provisions onto the bank. *The boat entered the Mississippi River at Cairo, Illinois, continuing northward past Saint Louis and as far as the steamboat could go.*

At Keokuk, Iowa some in our party walked 12 miles along the Mississippi to the head of the rapids. We who were unable to walk that distance rode on an open flatboat along with the boxed household goods. It was a cold, windy November day when horses, wading in the water, pulled this boat upstream. Arriving at Montrose we lodged overnight in the barracks of a long, log building. While awaiting a steamer from the north to come for us, we walked a way into the country. We found two graves that wolves had dug into trying to get at the bodies. Next day the steamer came and took us from Montrose to our landing place in the Iowa Territory.

In the beginning (1834) Congress established two large Iowa Territory counties. They were called Dubuque and Des Moines. As settlement increased, new counties were carved from these two. In 1836 Muscatine, Louisa, and Lee counties along the Mississippi, and Van Buren and Henry were organized. Lee county land had been opened for settlement in 1833, but Iowa's first school had opened near Montrose in October 1830 for the children of Dr. Isaac Galland. He was one of the white settlers who was permitted to live in the half-breed tract west of the Mississippi River. In 1837 Clayton, Jackson, Clinton, and Scott were organized along the Mississippi, and ten inland counties were added. The inland counties were Benton, Buchanan, Cedar, Delaware, Fayette, Linn, Johnson, Jones, Keokuk, Washington. Jefferson county was added in 1839, followed in 1843 by Blackhawk, Davis, Iowa, Poweshiek, Tama, Wapello. All other counties to the west came later.

Iowa Territory Expansion

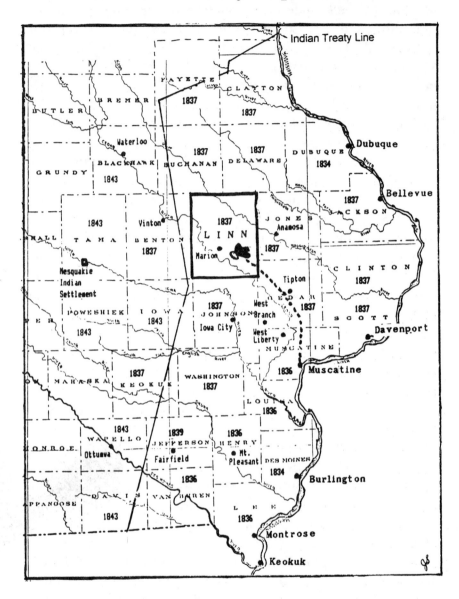

Map shows westward progression as counties were organized between 1834 and 1843. Linn was one of 14 counties organized in 1837. Andrew Kramer's footpath across two counties in the Iowa Territory shows route he first traveled in 1838 from Muscatine on the Mississippi to Linn Grove (shaded).

3   First Homes

Eastern Iowa had timber for building cabins

WE reached Bloomington on 8 November 1839 having traveled more than a thousand river miles in seven weeks. The city has been called Muscatine since 1849. In 1839 it was a city of six modest houses. A little house owned by a bachelor was secured for the two families for overnight. Our household goods were stored at a cost of twenty-seven dollars, two more than Father had. *Muscatine has had three names. Platted as Newburg in 1836, the name was soon changed to Bloomington, the post office 1839-1849* (Mott, p. 96). *In February 1839 Bloomington had a mostly male population of 71. Its 33 buildings included dwellings, stores, shops, and stables* (Jack, p. 10). *Finally the town was given an Indian name that means 'dwellers in the prairie'* (Hills, p. 12).

That afternoon Father walked 10 miles to Mr. Beaty's home, taking along two sons and two daughters. He arranged for Mr. Beaty to take the rest of us by wagon out to his house. Next morning Father and those with him continued walking to Linn Grove where his son Lewis had put up a cabin. Mr. Beaty came to Muscatine that morning and first attended his own business. It was nearly dark when he came to load us and the necessary goods. Meanwhile, a great cloud had arisen in the West. Before we reached the hilltop that now forms part of the city, the rain burst upon us in great sheets. The darkness and rain forced us to go back into town, picking our way through the mud and rain by flashes of lightning.

The owner of the house was not there, so we went in and occupied it again. It was small and leaky. The floor had a gentle slope from one side to the other. Beds were made up on the floor. It happened that mine was made on the lower side, and I 'slept' in two or three inches of water that night.

Early next morning my little sister was crying from hunger. Perhaps I cried, too. Mother refused to start without getting us something to eat. She gave Mr. Lutz a 'picayune' as six and one-fourth cent pieces were called. He tried to buy some bread, but no one would sell him any. Mother then took the money and, with the crying child in her arms, succeeded in getting a small loaf. We had breakfast before starting out on our 10-mile trip in an openmouthed prairie schooner.

The storm had cleared, leaving behind two or three inches of snow and a cold, penetrating northwest wind. Our family of six arrived at Beaty's home about noon. Near his house was a hazel patch; a scattering of burrs with nuts was still hanging on the bushes. This was something new to me, and of great interest. *Isaac was learning at a tender age to appreciate the produce of a bountiful earth.* We remained at Mr. Beaty's home until Father sent Lewis after us.

The trip to our new home was a cold one; the northwest wind swept into the open end of the schooner. We landed in Linn Grove on 18 November 1839. The claim was about one mile east of Lincoln road where it crossed Big Creek *(later called Lincoln Highway or US 30).*

Linn Grove was a distinct, extensive locality in the eastern part of Linn County. The grove itself, *about 7,000 acres,* extended over several townships. North Linn and South Linn Grove, as they were called, contained large tracts of timber. North Linn had the larger grove that extended up north and northeast from the Lincoln highway. It included country around Paralta and Springville. South Linn followed a ridge that ran eastward six miles or more from the road crossing over Big Creek. A prairie about two miles wide separated South

Linn from Sugar Grove. The land surface along Big Creek and eastern Linn Grove was rather hilly.

The three families, now united as one, shared the small cabin Lewis had built. Fifteen persons lived a while in this cabin that was 16-feet square, including the thickness of the walls. Half of the cabin had a puncheon floor made with slabs of split logs, slightly smoothed with an axe on the upper side. The other half of the floor was dirt. An open doorway was wide enough to admit a yoke of oxen hauling in large logs against which a fire could be built. Such openings were usually 'closed' by hanging up quilts or blankets, but it was soon found necessary to close the openings permanently. The opening was closed with logs, and big fire logs were 'walked in' through a smaller doorway. Chimneys were built of split slats or sticks on the outside against the log wall, and plastered with mud. Exposed places were constantly watched and plastered to keep them from catching fire.

Mr. Hiram Thomas' claim adjoined ours on the east. He had arrived the previous year and raised a little corn in the summer of 1839. His claim was a regular camping ground for Indians in the summer. A few weeks after we arrived, Father moved his family of eight to a small cabin on a claim that had been vacated east of the Thomas claim. It was called the Osborn cabin and perhaps did not exceed 10-feet square inside. A blanket was put up to do door service. *The Robert Osborn cabin was built in March 1838. It was the birthplace that September of the county's first white child. Her name was Maria Osborn* (1878 history, p. 344).

Here our family endured several of its most severe trials. My sister Charlotte was born in that cabin 20 December 1839, and my older brother, Michael, then past nine years of age, cut his foot with an axe. The serious wound laid him up for some time.

My sister Ann gave birth to a daughter, Christina, on 30 December 1839 at the Lewis Kramer home. *The Lutz family soon moved to a claim in what became Kenwood, midway between Marion and Cedar Rapids. They first lived in a little hut that had been built 'of poles and prairie grass' by Mr. David*

Jewell (Carroll, p. 16).

Within a few more weeks, Father traded a gun for a claim that was two miles farther east, near the middle of South Linn Grove. The gun was valued at about twenty-five dollars. The claim had a large cabin that was poorly chinked and plastered. Much of the plaster had fallen off. When we succeeded in getting some unfrozen dirt to make a mud plaster, continual freezing prevented it from sticking. Father moved his family into this cabin toward the end of January 1840.

After the move Father returned to Muscatine to get his goods. A heavy snow—10 inches or more—fell after he left. We were soon without a supply of wood. A neighbor, Mr. George A. Yeisley of Pennsylvania, discovered our predicament and cut down an oak tree near the door. *Yeisley, his wife, and their first child also had arrived in November 1839* (Clarke, p. 299). *Mr. Yeisley was an experienced lumberman.* He cut up most of the wood and carried the heaviest pieces into the house; we children dragged in the lighter portions.

Here we were in wild Indian country. Weird winds moaned and screeched, sweeping in cold waves over the seared earth. Wolves howled on the prairies and lynx screamed in the woods. We were without food, without money, and nine persons to feed.

Chimney is made of split sticks and plastered with mud

4   Faith and Perseverance

Mother working by lamplight

FATHER somehow managed to trade household goods for corn or cornmeal. However, we often had nothing to eat. On one occasion in Father's absence, we children prevailed on Mother to search the provision box in which food had been kept during our keelboat trip two months earlier. She found a biscuit so hard that it took an axe to divide it among three of us. Another time we coaxed Mother to cook some of the seed beans she had brought from Pennsylvania for planting. Many times we were destitute and knew not from whence our next meal would come.

Game was available but catching it required some skill in hunting and much ammunition. Ammunition was scarce and could not be had without money to buy it. Deer were plentiful, but white men did not often capture them unless expert at hunting. There were a few elks. Pheasants and wild turkeys were more numerous. Squirrels and prairie chickens were plentiful, but the country was not yet sufficiently 'civilized' for rabbit and quail.

During that first winter we saw no quail at all, and I heard of only one rabbit being found by all the men who made a business of hunting. In a few years both rabbit and quail were plentiful. My brother, Andrew, killed about a hundred prairie chickens during the first winter. We probably divided the birds among the three families; it helped a great deal.

It was during this time, I believe, that Father obtained some corn. The nearest mill was at Cascade in Dubuque county, 40 miles away. He took most of it there to be ground but found that the mill was six weeks behind with its grinding. He hauled the corn two miles to a barn for storing while awaiting its turn. At the appointed time he returned and took it to the mill. In the meantime three mills at home had been grinding busily to keep the Kramer family supplied with corn meal. Two of the grinders were coffee mills. The third was a medicine mortar made of cast iron that formed the lower millstone. Without a pestle, an iron wedge made for splitting rails simulated the upper millstone.

Settlers brought with them cooking utensils, surplus clothing material, and flax, wool, and woolen yarn. Some had wheels for spinning wool and flax, and hand cards for carding wool. In those days people did not mind having patched clothes. I remember hearing one man boast that his warm pants were made warmer by nine thick patches.

Jacob Mann was known for wearing patches. This colorful miller came to the county in February 1838 with his sons and a daughter, Sally. The daughter later raised and sold cats to the settlers. Marvin Oxley's unpublished typescript "Old Water Mills of Linn County" recalls a story his uncle told

> *One of the Oxley women spoke to Jakey in her customary straightforward manner. 'I want you to get another suit of clothes. Patch on top of patch is more than I can stand, and what makes it worse, they are all different colors.'*

> *Jakey replied in his native Carolina dialect: 'I'd liefer have a patch on my rear than a writ on the door.' His speech was as colorful as his clothing.*

Many times I saw my mother patching and darning by the midnight lamp, often falling asleep at her work. The lamp consisted of a cast-iron cup or saucer with a depression on one side for a spout, and on the other side a stem and hook to hang it up. Almost any kind of a rag would serve for a wick, laid in the spout and down on the bottom of the saucer. The lighted wick kept the lard melted to fuel the flame.

We children never realized the great stress laid on our parents. We truly did not understand the great faith and perseverance that enabled them to bear up so well under so many trying circumstances.

Isaac's Parents
Married in 1829

Andrew Kramer

1790 - 1872

Mary (Franks) Kramer

1801 - 1877

5   Claim Rights

George Greene: man of vision and action

George Greene, an Englishman from New York state, came to Davenport in 1838, and arrived in Linn county in 1839. At the age of 22 he taught school at Ivanhoe before he became Marion's first attorney. He traveled about the Territory and recognized that the people were ill-prepared to travel to the land office in Dubuque to enter their claims. The snow was deep and winter clothing to wear on such a trip was scarce, as was money to pay for the land.

Greene saw a way to improve the situation. He went to Washington City to ask that the land office be moved to Marion for March 1843 business. At the capital he called on three key officials: the commissioner of public lands, the chairman of the committee on territories (Stephen A. Douglas), and President John Tyler. He returned with an order for the temporary removal in his pocket, according to Samuel W. Durham's papers.

Durham had come from Vallonia, Indiana in 1840. Descended from a pioneer Kentucky family, he was blessed with near total recall and he lived a long life. Some of his writings, kept in the state archive at Iowa

City, add interesting anecdotes to the early history. A surveyor by trade, Durham bought much land himself. All public land was surveyed by private surveyors, like Durham, before it was offered for sale (from 1836 through 1859 in Iowa). Surveyors and their helpers tramped over the land and recorded their calculations. As a measuring device they used an iron chain with 100 links that extended 66 feet long. Ten square chains made an acre. The numbering system they used identifies townships, ranges, and sections. A base line through Little Rock, Arkansas was used for numbering congressional townships to the north. The fifth principal meridian forms the eastern boundary of Linn County and ranges are numbered west from it.

Some tracts of Iowa land came into market in the summer of 1840, but Linn County lands did not reach market until March 1843. The temporary Marion land office was located in a brick house owned by William H. Woodbridge, an enterprising young businessman who would die in the Mexican War. Preempting a claim involved asserting a right to title by reason of having settled on and improved the land. A series of general preemption acts permitted persons to buy public land at the minimum price of $1.25 an acre. The government paid about three cents an acre for territory that was part of the Louisiana Purchase. It paid additional fees to the tribes who possessed the land (Black Hawk Purchase).

The land sales drew many people to Marion from all the surrounding counties. It made lively times here, especially for hotel keepers Joseph F. Chapman and Oliver S. Hall. People with money got title to their lands. Those without cash held their claims until they could enter them at private sale. Adequate money was available for borrowing, and few settlers lost their claims. In the spring of 1843, the land office was moved back to Dubuque.

Now we return to Isaac's story.

CLAIM rights in the beginning were merely squatter rights. The government recognized the settlers' priority right to the land on which they had settled. However, claim jumping became quite a business. Gangs of roughs (claim jumpers) sometimes ousted new settlers and took possession by throwing out household goods, and turning women and children out-of-doors. Law abiding citizens organized to protect one another and soon put a stop to such raiding.

Some claim disputes were settled in a friendly way. Onalee Arnold provides an example from her family research. Her ancestor, Rufus H. Lucore, asserted his rights when Ira Leverich jumped his claim in Marion township. Leverich gave up the claim, and Mr. and Mrs. Lucore extended neighborly hospitality by inviting Leverich to share their home until he could find a suitable claim.

Our claim had a little neck of prairie nearly surrounded by timber. The plan was to grow wheat on these three acres the

View of this neck of prairie from cabin

first year. Rails had to be cut and split in the woods and hauled out to the prairie where the fencing was needed. This little patch required about 1,300 rails. Cutting and preparing these rails was a considerable task for the latter part of January and February. We had our small piece of prairie broken up, fenced, and sowed to wheat by 1 May. It was harvested by 1 August. The wheat was cut with a hand sickle and threshed with a hickory pole that had been limbered by pounding two and one-half feet from the heavy end. So prepared, the pole made an ideal flail while it lasted. After threshing, the wheat was winnowed by natures' ever-present fanning mill. *The wind removed chaff from the grains of wheat.* Some of the harvest was ground into flour, and from that time on we had wheat bread, a food we had not enjoyed for eight or nine months.

Mr. Hiram Beales, a bachelor, was our neighbor. He was famous as a hunter and for his good relations with the Indians. His claim was west of ours and contained three quarter-sections. Half of his 480 acres was timber, half prairie. He contracted to let the Indians have all the carcasses of the animals he killed. He was to keep the hides. For convenience, he left the carcasses on the cabin roof where the Indians could get them at any time. Sometimes the carcasses were left so long that they began to crawl, but the Indians never failed to take them. Although he tacked hides all over the outside walls of his cabin for drying, the Indians never took any of his skins.

In the spring of 1840, a distant relative, Mr. George Kramer from Morgantown, Virginia *(West Virginia since 1863)* came to see the country. He was pleased with Mr. Beales' chosen land and paid $400 for the claim right. It was a high price. George Kramer bought the claim for speculation and offered Father a seven-year lease with privilege of renewal for occupying and caring for the land. He required only such improvements as Father saw fit to make for his own benefit. Father had no prospect of paying for his own claim when it came to market. He gladly accepted. Some land had been broken, and I think we obtained immediate use of it. Mr. Beales did not move out for some time, and we remained on our own claim until he left.

When Mr. Beales moved to Marion, *probably in the fall of 1840,* he entered into partnership with Mr. Richard Thomas, better known as 'Uncle Dickie.' In the arrangement of their business, Mr. Beales came into possession of 160 acres of land, mostly on the west side of Indian Creek where the two men built a sawmill.

Marvin Oxley describes the site of this first sawmill, and a gristmill added later, in his typescript (Mills, 20-21)

A half mile or so west of the Marion business section, Indian Creek furnished a favorable power site. Two lengthy northern branches came together and followed a straight course for a time before passing through a rough, wooded area on its way to the Cedar River. Hiram Beales lost no time in taking squatter's title to this power site. He constructed a dam and put a sawmill in operation in 1841. David Styles, a millwright from Connecticut, helped build and install the machinery for the gristmill in 1843-44. The first pole bridge in the county was over the creek, and provided access from Marion to the mills.

Richard Thomas, who owned lands adjoining those of Beales, has always been associated with the gristmill where he was one of the millers. Thomas was born in Maryland and, at an early age, bound out to an uncle who mistreated him. He had witnessed the burning of Washington, D. C. by the British in 1814, migrated to Iowa Territory in 1838. Before returning to Marion in April 1840, he visited in Little Rock, Arkansas. While helping to build the sawmill, Thomas, age 58, endured a serious injury. The accident was caused when he fell into the water wheel while it was in motion. The rim of the wheel caught his right arm at the elbow and crushed it to the wrist, nearly drowning him. "By almost superhuman strength he stopped the wheel, while he instructed a fellow workman on how to extricate him. It would have resulted in the loss of his arm had he not stubbornly refused to allow the doctors to amputate. He recovered use of his arm so perfectly that no man in the region could successfully compete with him at work (Chapman, 389)." Another early sawmill, probably also in 1841, was built by Rufus Lucore on the east side of the Cedar River near Palo (Arnold).

A few years after we had moved from our own claim to the former Beales claim, Mr. Freeman Smith bought and occupied my father's claim. *Smith and his family of eight came from*

20

New Geneva, Pennsylvania in 1843. About this time the government was ready for the preemption of claims. George Kramer sent his son to preempt his claim. Young Kramer hired two of Mr. Smith's sons to put up a little cabin in which he slept one night to fulfill the legal requirement. He then traveled to Dubuque and preempted the claim. *An abstract of original land entries shows that George Kramer bought 160 acres in Linn township—half in February 1843, half in December 1845.*

During the winter of 1842-43, preceding the opening of land sales, Mr. Kramer sent eleven hundred dollars to pay the government price and other expenses of his claim. The nearest point to which he could send the money was Burlington, and Father went after it on horseback. While he was gone, the weather became stormy and bitterly cold. Father was delayed much longer than expected. The family feared that outlaws might have obtained some clue to the nature of his business, and was uneasy until he returned without mishap.

Early sowing was done by hand before 1 May

Men hunted wild birds and animals to provide food

6 Raising a Cabin

Dragging and stacking logs for a cabin

IT did not seem possible to the earliest settlers that prairie land two miles from timber could ever be settled. They built their cabins in the edge of timberland for protection from high winds and for convenience. An extensive amount of fencing was needed. Having timber close by was important. After choosing a building site, the settler went into the woods, selected suitable trees a foot or more in diameter, felled them, and cut them into lengths, generally 16 feet long. Using a yoke of oxen and log chain, he dragged each log to the building site. When the logs were readied and in one place, neighbors turned out to help raise the cabin. The logs were heavy. Skids and spiked poles enabled the pioneers to stack logs to the required height. An axe man on each corner received and fitted each log. Fitting was accomplished by hewing the upper side of the log on both sides making an apex and notching a cut on the under side of the next log to fit over it. This technique bound the building at the corners.

Whiskey flowed freely and often made dangerous work of cabin raising. The gang of men at each end of the log raced to get their end in place and risked throwing one end off the skid. Another danger occurred when all the men let go at once before the corner men had the log firmly in command. At one raising, a son told the people his father had joined the church 14 times. This angered the father who insisted he had joined only 13 times. Probably drink had a lot to do with the vehemence displayed, to the disgust of many.

While these cabins had doorways, they did not always have doors, and window openings did not always have glass windows. Light cloth at windows served to let in a little daylight while keeping out a little cold. Nearly all the early cabins were the same size; sometimes the settlers put up two cabins close together. They chinked cracks between logs with pieces of split timber driven tightly and fastened with hard sharp wooden pins. Cracks were also daubed with common earth mixed with dry prairie grass.

The axe was the principal tool for building. It was used in place of a saw and hammer for cutting and driving. Making doors and roofing required a froe, gimlet, auger, saw and hammer, draw knife, foot adze, and broad axe.

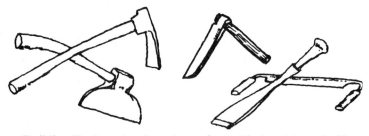

Building Tools: adze, broad axe, froe, chisel and draw knife

Roofs were made of clapboards about three feet long, rived (split) from oak timber, and laid on without shaving. These clapboards were laid lengthwise on poles, and fastened with wooden pins as the gable ends were put up. A second layer was lapped over the upper end of the first layer. It was fastened by pinning a pole over the laps of each tier and one on each side of the comb at the top.

Doors were made of lumber split like the clapboards, only longer. They were shaved with a draw knife and fastened with wooden pins to cleats that were thicker at one end to accommodate the hinge. The latch was a wooden blade fastened loosely with a string tied on one end. The other end protruded through a hole above the latch and served to open the door from outside. This was the proverbial latch string that was said to be always hanging out as a sign of welcome.

When upper rooms were added to cabins, joists were made of slim, straight poles (generally pig nut). For flooring, the bark off two linden logs about 2 1/2-feet in diameter were sufficient to cover the whole room. Laid with the inside down and weighted to keep from curling up, the bark served for both floor and ceiling. The stairway consisted of a hole in the floor with a ladder providing access. These upper rooms had but little headroom. As soon as the lumber was available for floors, the cabins were built higher and the upper story used for sleeping apartments where boys could study astronomy through cracks in the roof.

Clapboard roof is made from oak timber

24

7 Keeping House

Iron kettles hang from hooks over hearth fire

THE old-fashioned fireplace warmed the home, cooked the food, and provided light. With a pair of andirons supporting the ends, a blazing fire was kindled against big back logs piled three high. Any settler who failed to bring along andirons used stones in their place.

The hearth was made of flat stones, when they could be had, laid flat on the ground. If such stones were not available, the ground made do for a hearth. The fireplace occupied space mostly outside the cabin. The wall was cut out to make way for it. The outside wall and two end walls (jams) were built of stone to protect from fire. The stick chimney, laid up like a bird trap (cage) of split sticks, rose up against the outside wall and was plastered with mud on the inside.

The left-side jam accommodated two firmly built iron eyelets. These supported an iron crane that could swing back and forth over the fire with the suspended cooking utensils. Kettles were made of cast iron with cast-iron lids. Even tea kettles were cast iron. Skillets and pans were not intended for suspension. Pots, kettles, and baking ovens had eyes on either side to receive the movable pot hooks or bales required for suspending them on the crane over the fire. Besides the bales, movable hooks of different lengths were used to lengthen or shorten the distance from the fire as needed. Bread was baked in large pots or ovens with flat bottoms placed upon the coals; coals were also placed on the lids to bake the top of the bread.

Our parents brought with them another utensil for baking bread—the Reflector. It had an iron frame about fifteen inches high on which pans of dough were set to bake. The pans were probably sheet iron. A top frame above was probably ten or twelve inches high in front and perhaps less than half that on the back. A sheet of tin covered this frame on top and extended down behind to the pan frame. Another tin plate underneath the bread pans slanted upward toward the back. The ends were closed up with tin plate and the wide front left open. When the open side was set before the fire, the tin reflected heat from below and downward over the bread, baking both sides quite evenly. However, the Reflector had baked better before a Pennsylvania grate coal fire than before the typical wood fire in Iowa.

We had no stoves in those days. The first stove I ever saw was a box stove used for heating the schoolhouse. This was several years after we came to Iowa. Several years more passed before cook stoves of the rudest kind were introduced. *A Burlington newspaper advertisement in 1843 offered an assortment of stoves.* I do not remember seeing a match until about six years after we came to Iowa. Father brought them from Saint Louis. They were made of cloth and saturated with oil. Not more than one in every twenty-five would strike a blaze when rubbed on a specially prepared surface. Quite a difference from the matches carried about in the pocket in 1919.

The early settlers had not even that advantage, if advantage it was. Pioneers had to obtain their fire from sun, wood, or flint; perhaps flint was the most common. Many settlers had flintlocks on their guns. A little powder scattered on the flash pan took fire when the flint was struck, and the spark flew off into the powder. This in turn set fire to a substance called punk, a kind of fungus that grows in decaying wood. When it is dry, punk ignites easily. Punk was often carried about in the pocket to be used for this purpose.

Because such devices were not practical for daily use, people kept fire overnight and even for a day or two by covering live coals with ashes. When the coals failed to keep the required time, "borrowing" fire was common. For neighbors who lived two or three miles apart, borrowing was less satisfactory. However, cast-iron cooking utensils were handy for carrying, and the fire could be kept alive by adding fuel. Large beds of banked coals in the wintertime presented no difficulty in keeping fire overnight, but occasionally a mishap or long absence from home made borrowing necessary.

Bedsteads consisted of four rails fastened to four posts of proper dimensions. The supporting rails had holes bored in them every eight or ten inches. The many little holes furnished a hiding place for bugs. Little pins turned with heads on them held the rope in place from end to end and side to side. Much manipulation and stretching made the rope tight, forming springs on which to lay the mattress. The mattress could be a straw tick or featherbed. The size of the room determined the number of bedsteads.

Bed clothing consisted mainly of patch quilts and blankets with featherbeds and straw ticks. When the family was large, some beds were made on the floor alongside trundle beds that could be pushed under the higher full-size ones. A cradle completed the bed list. It might have been brought from the fatherland or homemade out of a sugar trough *(scooped out log for catching maple sugar water)* with rockers attached. It might be a half-piece of hollow log with the ends nailed up.

Our furniture in those early days included a bureau or two, a rough cupboard for dishes, a table, or goods' boxes when no table was available. Chairs and boxes provided seating. Pins driven into the log walls served for hanging guns or clothes. Shelves set on pins around the walls were useful.

The blazing hearth fires furnished light for working, reading, and studying on a winter evening. These fires also induced isolated settlers to foster an extensive system of evening visiting. Visitors would stay until midnight when keeping up lively talk of experiences and difficulties. The evening always ended with long 'ghost' stories that made the hair of the young listening Americans 'stand on end.'

Townships within a County

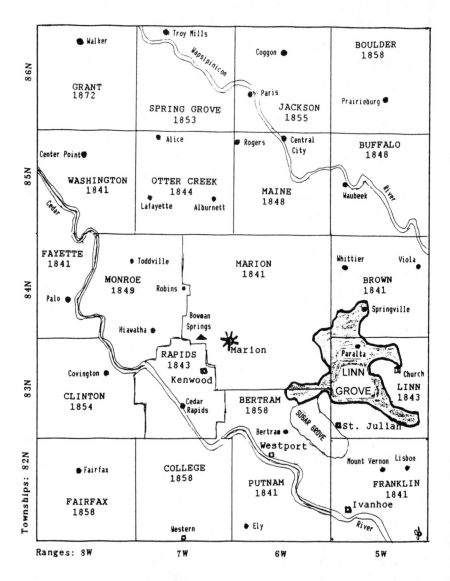

Counties were politically organized into townships to bring government closer to the settlers. Map locates rivers, towns, and shows year townships were formed in Linn County. Two early settlements (Westport and Ivanhoe) did not survive. Linn Grove south (lower right) was Isaac Kramer's boyhood home.

Brick courthouse at Marion served from 1846 to 1925

Iowa's oldest towns sprang up along the Mississippi in the early 1830s, Dubuque in the north, and Davenport and Burlington in the southern part of the Territory. Settlers pushed ever westward seeking claims on virgin land, and first reached Linn County in 1836. The county was not organized until 1837. Two large rivers dissect the county: the Cedar cuts across the southwestern part, and the Wapsipinicon slices through the northeast. Linn County also has dozens of creeks that provide handy water for drinking, bathing, and washing clothes.

The first four towns in Linn County were Westport (July 1838), Columbus on the western bank of the Cedar River (September 1838), Ivanhoe (October 1838), and Marion (April 1839). Columbus later became part of west Cedar Rapids. Marion is the only survivor among these first four. Its location near the center of the county was judged ideal for the county seat in 1839. Territorial Governor Robert Lucas appointed commissioners who met in March at William Abbe's log cabin home. They chose Marion because it was accessible to voters and the *site was thought to promote good health. The Federal census of 1840 counted more than 1,300 Linn county citizens in some 250 households, and by 1844 the population had nearly doubled. Isaac's story continues.*

WHEN Father visited Iowa Territory in 1838 *Linn County had a total population of 205;* Westport and Ivanhoe were the most important towns. These towns no longer exist, but in the fall of 1838 Andrew Kramer met many persons at Westport *where Albert Henry had opened the first store.* From other claim prospectors he got the impression that Westport was the central meeting place for the county. It was located where Big Creek enters the Cedar River in the southern part of the county.

While Father was at Westport, a man called him out privately and proposed a partnership in making bogus. Father did not know what bogus meant. The man *(Joel 'Jo' Leverich)* explained that out of $100 silver he could make four hundred that would pass *(be accepted)* at the land office. Father told him that he did not engage in such business. It is supposed that this man—who had a great reputation as a bogus maker and was known as the 'old bogus coon'—believed Father had considerable money. If so, he had plans for getting hold of it. *As reported in the first chapter, Andrew Kramer had suffered a devastating financial setback in 1837. He had no savings, and was seeking a fresh but honest start for his family in the new territory. He sold or exchanged personal belongings for necessities.*

By December of 1846, when Iowa became the twentyninth state, Westport was a shipping port for wheat. Four flatboat loads were shipped from there and delivered to Saint Louis by way of the Cedar, Iowa, and Mississippi rivers. Father and others with their 1845 wheat crops on board went along to man the boats. *During the winter Robert Ellis had built three flatboats at Palo on the Cedar. They were 60 feet long, 16 feet wide, drawing three feet of water when loaded. In late March 1846, these boats took on four thousand bushels of wheat with three men on each to navigate bends in the rivers* (Brewer I, p. 424).

Westport's downfall came in the late 1850s. *Founded by Israel Mitchell in July 1838, Westport was renamed Newark in 1844, and faded some 20 years later.* I visited Westport only once—in the fall of 1840—when I was taken there to have clothes cut out by the tailor. He cut out and fitted clothing for settlers whose womenfolk did their own sewing. The railroad bypassed Westport. As a result the town of Bertram took its place some distance from the river.

The next town of importance was Ivanhoe. It was located five or six miles southwest of Mount Vernon on the Cedar River. *Ivanhoe was founded by Anson Cowles along the Territory's first road in October 1838. Cowles, an eccentric character who appreciated the novels of Sir Walter Scott, named the town for one of the novels. Colonel William H. Merritt opened the first store in Ivanhoe in 1839.*

Gillettsburg was located two miles south of Mount Vernon and six miles from our home. *The town is not listed among Iowa's abandoned towns, probably because* it met death in its infancy and had only a store, one house, and a barn in the zenith of its glory. I would never have known Gillettsburg existed except that my brother and I were sent there with two horse-loads (sacks full) of wheat to trade for groceries. On our return the sacks were not nearly so full.

In making this trip we passed near the site of Mount Vernon. Whether that was before Mount Vernon was born or because Gillettsburg traded in wheat and Mount Vernon did not, I cannot say. I do have some memories of Mount Vernon's unhappy early days. One businessman advertised his wares with a bean of coffee strung on a pinhook. Afterward the whole town was thought to be a Pinhook. When Mr. *Rev. George B.* Bowman started his college enterprise the town fast outgrew that appellation.

Other towns that started up in the early day were Center Point *in 1839; Springville started in 1842, Paris by Samuel Justine, and Lafayette with John Nevin's sawmill, both in 1845. Center Point was originally called McGonigle's Point.* No other towns can be classed as originating with the earliest settlers.

William Abbe who lived from 1800 to 1854 appears to be the county's first settler. He brought his family from Ohio in 1837 to the claim he staked in 1836. It was located on Abbe's Creek in northwest Franklin township. Later in 1837 Charles C. Haskins settled in the Lisbon-Mount Vernon area, and Edward M. Crow of Indiana chose the Viola area as his home. Each man picked a spot that suited his fancy. Lisbon was platted in 1851 following the arrival in 1847 of a colony from Pennsylvania. Joseph Chapman first made claim on the Mount Vernon site in 1842, and is the older settlement (Chapman, pp. 956-959).

Three different buildings served as courthouses in Marion. Volunteer laborers constructed the first building with logs in 1840-1841. The Methodist church used this building after a new frame structure replaced it as the courthouse. The third building was constructed of brick beginning in 1843. Completed in 1846 it served as the county's courthouse for 79 years. It was on the site, opposite City Park Square, where in 1996 the new Marion library is being built. (Onalee Arnold documented the years of construction from records of the Linn County Commissioners' account books dated July 1843, April and July 1844, and January and July 1846.) County population had grown to 3,411 by 1846, the year Iowa achieved statehood.

William K. Farnsworth was said to be the first 'settler' in Marion although he did not build the first house there. That task fell to Luman M. Strong who arrived in the county early in 1839. Strong built the first house and inn near Indian Creek on Central avenue (Alburnett road). Although built of hewn logs, "the inn was finished up on the outside like a frame house, and had an upper and lower porch facing town (east). There was nothing else so elaborate in central Iowa in 1840." Strong hauled materials (lumber, glass, and nails) for the inn from Rock Island. Many businessmen who came in the early years made the inn their home (Oxley).

Marion and Cedar Rapids soon became the leading

towns, and keen rivalry between the two developed during the first six years of their dual existence. Their centers are six miles apart. The county seat had been located at Marion before the Kramers arrived. It was a beautiful and healthy location and Marion gained ascendancy for a while. Cedar Rapids was surveyed and platted as Rapids City, and lagged behind until the Cedar River was harnessed to furnish power for mills and factories. The first railroad gave Cedar Rapids additional advantage, and the city soon surpassed Marion in growth and importance. However, Cedar Rapids did not win the county seat contest until 1919 following a 64-year battle.

Samuel Durham helped survey Rapids City in August 1841. It was soon renamed Cedar Rapids. Durham wrote that he helped lay out First Street as it is now called

It was 100 feet wide, parallel with the river, and along its bank. Then they laid out First Avenue or Iowa Avenue, as they called it, 120 feet wide, at right angles with First Street. This was aimed to be the most important thoroughfare—as State Street is to Chicago or Pennsylvania Avenue to Washington City. The company [owners of the land that became downtown Cedar Rapids] donated land for the unusually wide streets and alleys.

When this survey was made there were but two houses on the east side of the river. Osgood Shepard and Asher Edgerton occupied them. I have eaten and slept in both. Shepard was a lively, red haired fellow.

Another professional man wrote about Cedar Rapids as it looked in 1849 when he first saw it, eight years after the survey. Dr. Seymour D. Carpenter recalled his conversation with Judge George Greene in Ottumwa where they had met when Greene was a member of the Supreme Court of Iowa.

He persuaded me that Cedar Rapids was soon to become a metropolis and I decided to go there. After four days' hard riding and swimming several swollen streams, I struck the town on the afternoon of 14 June 1849. I crossed the river on a rope ferry operated by David King who lived in a cabin on the west side. On the other side of the river stood a cabin once the home of a man named Shepard. The cabin was said to be the resort of thieves in an early day. I cannot say that I was favorably impressed by the 30 or 40 small one-story unpainted houses that were scattered about near the river. There seemed to be a great deal of sand, and the houses were so situated that there was no sign of a street.

The young doctor stayed, however, because he had only ten dollars in his pocket. The village of Cedar Rapids was first chartered in 1849, and organization began in earnest; the county's population increased by 1,282 persons that year. The doctor's father, Gabriel Carpenter (1801-1881), came from Lancaster, Pennsylvania in 1852 to help his son. The father invested his funds in five hundred acres of land that became the heart of downtown. The son soon gave up the practice of medicine to deal in railroad building, banking, and real estate.

Dr. Carpenter also wrote about one of the men Andrew Kramer had encountered at Westport eleven years earlier

I had hardly gotten settled at the Coffman Hotel until I was interviewed by old Joel Leverich, the noted character of Linn County of that day. He was known as the 'bogus coon' because, as was alleged, he had to do with counterfeiters.

Other historians also mentioned Joel Leverich. The 1878 history reports

Instead of using his extraordinary talents in legitimate ways, Joel chose to be the leader of a gang that preyed on society. He was, beyond question, the head center of the band of freebooters and counterfeiters. He never *stole horses or made bogus money, but his willing tools looked up to him as their guide and protector. He is described as a man of commanding presence, who could so impress those with whom he came in contact, that a piece of bad money would be taken from him without question.*

Rev. George Carroll wrote that "the notorious Joel Leverich" was known and dreaded, "especially when he was under the influence of liquor, which was often the case."

Dr. Carpenter concluded his reminiscences

I was with him (Leverich) when he died and, although he was a freethinker, he passed away with all the calmness of a stoic philosopher.

Someone said to him on his deathbed, 'Jo, you have burned the candle at both ends.'

'Yes,' he replied, 'and now it burns me in the middle.'

Electric streetcar travels east of Indian Creek along Marion Boulevard in the early 1900s. The Boulevard leads southwest to Cedar Rapids.

9   Early Roads

Settlers traveled across the prairie in schooners and on horseback

THE first settlers did not confine their travel to specific roads. They went in the direction they had to go; the prairie itself offered better opportunities and fewer obstacles. Bridges had not yet been built and worn tracks were abandoned for new ones. It was called cutting around, and the cutting around at such places sometimes made an extremely wide road.

A definite road evidently was marked out from Muscatine to Marion before we came to Iowa in 1839. As a direct route, it must have passed through the sites afterward occupied by Lisbon and Mount Vernon. A branch road from Ivanhoe connected with it, as did one reaching the eastern end of Linn Grove. Another road from Westport followed up the west side of Big Creek to the Muscatine-Marion road. At this place on Big Creek was a mill site used for a sawmill in 1844, then as a grist or flouring mill. A road from that point extended up into the lower part of Linn Grove. *Three brothers (James, Mark, and Prior Scott) owned the sawmill* (Oxley, Mills).

An early road from the west end of Linn Grove to Marion crossed Big Creek about a mile above Scott's Mill near the mouth of Elbow Creek. It was called the Davenport Road. Between the two ends of South Linn there was no permanent road connection until late in January 1840. Then a road was cut lengthwise through the grove's center leaving piles of logs and many stumps. The bridge across the creek was not built until long after the road was cut. *Surveyed by Samuel Durham,* the road was designed to connect Marion to Davenport, but it never amounted to a real public road.

A military road from Dubuque to Iowa City existed in the days of Black Hawk (famous Sak Indian war chief). It probably crossed the Maquoketa River at Cascade and the Wapsipinicon River near Anamosa, a little above the east end of Linn Grove. It is possible that a road from Marion connected with the Military Road, making a through road to Dubuque. The road was accessible to Linn Grove residents.

At an early date, a road leading northwest from Marion had no apparent destination. It crossed the Cedar River about seven miles from Marion where a ferry named for the builder was established. The road from Marion is still called Blairs Ferry Road. It seems to have no special destination except as a way for citizens living along it to get to and from Marion. *In the 1850s, Blair's Ferry road was a western route for travelers. An advertisement in the 31 December 1853 issue of the Marion Register said: "The subscriber (Albert Blair) has now in successful operation on the road from Marion to Vinton a new rope ferry. Emigrants and others wishing to go into counties west will find this the shortest route . . ." A new road was laid out, and instead of turning southwest to Usher's Ferry, this road turned gently northwest . . . running a short distance south of Palo. At times in the 1850s, a hundred wagons lined up waiting to cross the Cedar* (Oxley, I, p. 162).

It has been reported that the first road from Marion to Cedar Rapids started out in a northward direction on Tenth street by way of what was called Sulphur Springs. The first road from Marion to Cedar Rapids that I personally knew about was the one I traveled in the spring of 1840. I was going to Kenwood to visit my sister and brother-in-law, Ann and Barnet Lutz. Then, the road followed along where the streetcar line and road are in 1919. When it got well up the hill, the road turned southeastward. The detour toward Indian Creek was made to avoid two large ponds on the hill. In rainy spells water covered the ground between the two ponds but was not deep at any place. Finally a corduroy road was laid between the ponds, and travel turned that way. However, the road veered toward the creek until the street railway line was established.

When the corduroy road was built between the ponds, a culvert was added to carry water from the west pond across to the east side. Surplus water from both ponds was carried off down the hillside several rods east of the road. After damaging Mr. Twogood's field, the water flow followed down to the creek and, in time, washed out the roadside.

A. J. Twogood became Marion's leading drover after he came here from New York in 1852; he actively traded in land, livestock, and grain. Corduroy or plank roads were the first hard-surface highways built on Iowa soil. The first streetcars were powered by steam and horses; on the first day of operation in May 1880, "Passengers got out and pushed when necessary, and seemed to enjoy it." Streetcars were powered by electricity after 1891.

Isaac Kramer in 1867 obtained 15 acres along Marion Boulevard and established the first important plant and seed business in the county. He had married Sarah Flack and their son, Judson, then 5, later became Isaac's business partner. Isaac's business and home site had been part of Hiram Beales claim above the mill site. The road was first called Marion Boulevard in 1877 after county supervisors approved $20,000 to improve the roadway and made it 60-feet wide (Oxley, II, pp. 288-289).

The Milwaukee railroad track was laid from Marion to Cedar Rapids in 1865. The west pond was thoroughly drained, and all the surplus water was dumped onto property I later bought. After paying me for damages following the first heavy rain, the railroad got permission from Marion officials to dump the water on the Blairs Ferry Road instead of carrying it all the way to the creek on their own land. In 1919 the flood water follows the road along my place. It does some damage every year before it empties into the creek above the bridge, rather than below as it did before.

10   Taming the Prairie

Prairie breaking, a specialized occupation; farm boy (left) drops sod corn

PRAIRIE was the chosen land for cultivation. However, it was covered by grass with a network of tough fibrous roots. The roots were so thoroughly matted that breaking it required hitching three or four yokes of oxen to one plow. A single team could not break up the sod unless the grass had been pastured enough to weaken the roots. In that case a team of horses was sometimes used, but few settlers could do their own breaking.

The oxen had to make their own living by grazing at noon and during the nighttime. It was a matter of good policy to have a portion of prairie reserved to burn for late pasture. The new growth of grass that followed burning made good pasturage.

In truth prairie breaking became a specialized seasonable occupation. The most desirable season was from May to early July. Later on, as demand increased, the season was prolonged through the summer months. Average cost was $2.50 to $4 an acre with as high as $5 reported during the Civil War. Some-times board for the operator and his helper was included in the compensation (Ross, p. 56).

Two men that I knew made breaking prairie a business. They were Mr. Luther McShane and Mr. Calvin Newman. *When they arrived in 1840 with their respective parents, both were teenagers.* Mr. Newman broke about 80 acres for us one summer. He killed on average one rattlesnake to the acre. Although prairie breakers were more in danger of these snakes than any other people, I never heard of a prairie plowman being bitten. I have heard that several oxen used by the breakers suffered snake bites.

My own brother was bitten one early forenoon while walking barefoot through deep grass. He came right home where all the family engaged in gathering and pounding plantain. Bits of it were applied to the bite as soon as the bit was made ready, and Michael was able to walk out in the field in the afternoon of the same day.

One man managed both team and plow; the plow beam was attached to the axletree and two wheels of a wagon. One wheel ran in the furrow, the other on the unplowed sod. A lever, attached to the end of the beam, was held in place with a wooden pin. The lever controlled the depth of plowing. The lever could also throw the plow out of the ground when necessary. Because the plow was large, with its beam attached to the axletree, it was not easily thrown out of the ground except by moving the lever. The moldboard was made of steel rods rather than a continuous surface. The driver need pay but little attention to the plow except at the ends of the furrows. Then he would throw it out of the ground and, after turning, set it in again.

It was advisable not to plow deep, and it was best to have the plow shaped so that the sod would curl up into small peaks or cones. Thus turned up, the grass roots might dry out and die in the hot summer sun. The cones were easily harrowed down when thoroughly dried out, leaving the ground in good condition for putting in crops. It was remarkable how few weeds came up because none of the pests existed that now fill the soil.

Some of the earlier breaking was planted to sod corn, but most planting was postponed until the season following breaking. *Sometimes the farmer had his sons "drop corn along every third or fourth furrow." Sod corn required no cultivation and allowed the pioneer "more time to get situated his first summer." About thirty bushels to the acre could be expected* (Letterman, p. 75). The grain-raiser bore the expense of pasturing the cattleman's stock. All broken ground must be fenced before crops were planted.

'Worm fence' got its name from its zigzag appearance

Rail or worm fence, as it was usually called, was universally used for fencing. The rails were ten feet long, about five inches in diameter, cut and split in the woods during the winter and hauled out to the field to be fenced in early spring. White, oak, red oak, and white ash were the preferred trees for fencing rails. In mixed groves scarcely a third of the timber was suitable for rail fence. Fencing farmlands rapidly consumed all the good rail timber. The introduction of wire fencing and railroads came to our rescue. Railroads made it possible to haul lumber and alternative fuels into the state after 1860. Wire fencing saved much timber for other uses *(such as lumber and fuel)*. *Joseph F. Glidden of DeKalb, Illinois invented barbed wire in 1873.*

A single length of rail laid up into fence was called a panel. Laid at an angle the ends could be crossed on one another to build up height. It took two lengths of rails to lay one rod (16 1/2 feet) of fence. The fence row occupied a strip of ground about four feet wide because of the angling back and forth which gave it the name 'worm fence.'

A good rail fence would be laid five or six rails high and double ridered. Rails averaged about five inches in diameter. When laid up they made a crack the same size so each rail laid in a fence counted about ten inches. A five-rail fence would be about four feet high. Double riders for such a fence required two stakes for each panel or corner. One stake was set in the ground on either side, and the two were made to cross each other at the top of the corner. One end of another rail was laid in this cross, and the other end laid on the fence before the next two stakes were set. A second rail was laid on top of one in the cross of the stakes and the other end on the top rail in the next panel. A forty-acre field (320 rods around) would require about 4,500 rails and more than 1,250 stakes.

Laying fence for a good-sized farm made many hard jobs in winter and spring, and a great deal of labor was required to keep it in repair. Prairie fires destroyed thousands of rails that then had to be replaced.

The settlers universally agreed that whoever raised grain should fence against all kinds of farm animals—his own as well as that of his neighbors. *This belief was based on law—a Massachusetts order enacted in the 1640s.* The settlers did not see that it would have cost less to fence in the cattle, hogs, horses, and sheep whose continual straying required a great deal of hunting time. They presumed that everyone would acquire stock quickly. They accepted that such stock had a right to forage for food wherever they could find it, no matter who claimed or owned the land.

Under the charm of this sentiment, people for many years after could see the justice of every man being made to pay the expenses of his own property. By this arrangement the man too poor to own stock must confine himself to raising grain. At great expense to himself, he must fence it in to protect his neighbors' cattle from entering upon his land and destroying his crop. Thus the neighbors' cattle would be free to roam all unfenced land.

11   Farming Equipment

Sod buster plow broke the virgin prairie's tough roots

Most of the early settlers came to Iowa with team and wagon and brought other necessary tools with the family household goods and cooking utensils. Those who came by river, as my family did, had to buy team and wagon after arriving. A team, wagon, plow, and harrow were the first requirements for farming.

Newcomers brought wagons from all parts of the country. Some were homemade with wheels fashioned from the sawed-off ends of a log. One type of wagon was the six-horse mountain barge that had a large heavy box with high curved ends. Like two horns of a crescent at front and back, these barriers kept goods from rolling off as the barge went up or down mountain hills. Barges were not suitable for sailing in Iowa mud; they could not compete with the ordinary prairie schooner.

Some of the wagons served as respectable ox buggies fitted with removable seats called chairs that were borrowed from the house. These chairs were placed none too substantially in the middle of the wagon box. If two persons were to ride, the seats might go in side by side. The driver did not need a seat; he would be better down on the ground looking after the movements of the horse power. Often those who went buggy riding did not need any seats but instead sat flat down on a little straw or prairie hay.

Sometimes oxen decided to run fast. This generally resulted in uncomfortable buggy riding. On the other hand, the propelling power might include an old balky ox. When the notion came to balk, it was a regular breakdown—not unlike automotive breakdowns in the present year of 1919. While this was about as uncomfortable as the rapid transit, it was not nearly so dangerous.

Crude wagon pulled by ox team features sawed-off log wheels

The most important tool was the plow. Plows also came from everywhere. They were all shapes and kinds: wooden moldboards, rod moldboards, full-surface iron moldboards. Some large heavy cast-iron plows had moldboards that were convex in the middle, compared to 1919 plows that are concave. These and some others had a long curved extension to the upper corner of the moldboard with an apparent mission of laying the soil over flat and plastering it down.

This plow, like all the others, dragged through Iowa soil like a log and, when the soil was too damp, left it more crumbly. In that respect it left the soil in better condition than did the scouring plow. Cast-iron plows came with duplicate cast-iron points, and such plows might last the Iowa farmer at least a half dozen generations.

When steel scouring plows were introduced, all the cast-iron variety immediately disappeared. Perhaps they were melted down for cannon balls during the Mexican War *(1846-1848)* or for the three wars that have followed *(Civil 1861-1865, Spanish-American 1898-1899, First World War 1914-1918)*. I do not know who invented the scouring plow for the western soil, but it was manufactured by Andrew Safley near the Saint Julian post office in an early day. His were the best plows ever made for Iowa soil. *The Safleys came to the county in 1838 from Scotland.* After a few years when the Moline plow became available, he stopped making them. Mr. Safley did not care to engage in as large a business as the demand required. Although his plow cost five dollars more than the Moline plow, people were disappointed in not being able to get them. The Safley plow, with its steel share and moldboard, presented a half circle of smooth surface that apparently pressed the soil with equal force, and no spot of the surface failed to scour. Besides being larger, the Safley plow ran more smoothly than the Moline, and the upper hind corner of the moldboard was much shorter. *John Deere (1804-1886), a Vermont-born blacksmith, invented the steel plow from a circular saw blade in about 1837. Ten years passed before he established a plow works in Moline, Illinois to supply midwest farmers. The firm was incorporated as Deere and Company in 1868.*

Triangle harrow was made of tree limbs with iron teeth added

The old-fashioned harrow was made of three pieces of timber fastened together to form a triangle. Sometimes a small tree of the right size and properly branched was used to form two of the sides. Iron teeth were driven through auger holes in the frame at intervals of about ten inches. If harrow teeth were not available, the harrowing was accomplished by dragging brush over the ground.

Plow shovels, made specially for cultivating corn, were fashioned of triangular sheet steel with sides twelve to fourteen inches each. One point and two of the sides were sharpened and the point suitably curved. This shovel was bolted to a wood beam, and handles attached above with a wooden hitching pin at the other end.

**Double shovel plowed
on both sides of corn row**

**Horse hoe plowed
between corn rows**

The hand hoe was indispensable for covering corn and cutting weeds. It was then about the same shape as the 1919 variety. Instead of a shank, there was an eye in the hoe through which the handle was driven. Hoe blades made by the blacksmith were both clumsy and heavy, and the small hickory sapling used for a handle was continually working loose in the eye.

Wheat required other tools. Sickles or cradles cut it. Wooden rakes helped to gather it. Threshing machines—either hickory clubs or otherwise as they developed over time—separated the grain from stalks. Fanning mills were either of human manufacture or by nature's handiwork *(wind in the open air)*.

Tools for wheat: hand sickle cuts, flail threshes, fan removes chaff

12   Early Crops

Corn yields food for humans and animals

CROPS in the early years were mostly corn and wheat. Because markets were so far away, corn was not considered a cash crop. It sometimes brought only ten cents a bushel, and was costly to haul, but corn was considered a necessity. Corn furnished food for humans and all kinds of livestock. We depended on the wheat crop alone to bring in money.

Soil for corn was prepared by plowing and, if circumstances permitted, by harrowing. Then the soil was cross–furrowed with the broad shovel plow. The shovel plow could be pulled by one horse, releasing the second half of the team for other work. Another person was the dropper. Guided by stakes, the man or boy dropped corn kernels in the furrows with one hand. Using the hoe with his other hand, he covered the kernels. The stakes were generally made of young wood with the bark peeled off at the top. Peeling made them more visible in marking the width of the row.   This was not a fast operation, but an expert could drop six acres in a day. An experienced dropper who could keep up with the horse, dropped at least eight acres per day. Grown men received fifty cents per day; boys twenty-five cents. Corn was planted three and one-half feet apart and cultivated with the broad-shovel plow, two furrows to the row.

Because of my small size and weakly appearance, I was usually assigned the easiest part of the job. A man or boy walking behind the plow with lines over his shoulders to control the horse would firmly hold the plow in place by the two handles. Sometimes he wrapped a single line around his left wrist. The horse was taught to go left or right by voice command and, when necessary, a gentle pull on the line signaled a left turn while a quick short jerk or two meant "go to the right." Five acres twice in the row was a normal day's work for a man and horse. Occasionally an ox would replace the horse with lines fastened to his horns.

We always expected to have the corn laid by by the Fourth of July. As soon as corn was three-fourths dented, men went to the field to gather seed corn. They took it to the cabin home for husking. Then they put it up over the kitchen fire to dry. Corn became blackened by the smoke and appeared unfit even for hog feed. Old settlers knew what was in those smoky kernels. I have seen such unpromising-looking corn planted side by side with good, well-ripened corn; the smoky corn came up more quickly and grew faster by at least a week.

In 1919 we have larger, finer houses but no tolerance for unsightly seed corn in the home. Most farmers could have a small building fitted up for this purpose, but this would cost too much in time and bother for these automobile-riding days. One man alone might put up such a building and dry corn for several neighbors, and charge twenty-five percent of the cost of a bushel. However, that man would be making too much money off his neighbors to be tolerated. I suppose the world will continue on as it is going.

Double-cross hybrid seed corn was made available to farmers as early as 1921, but hybrid seed did not displace the old standard strains until the early 1940s. Hybrid seed corn requires special handling in growing and harvesting. These tasks are not readily accomplished by the average farmer. Since 1943 farmers buy the seed needed for planting each year. Iowa's Henry A. Wallace, vice president of the United States from 1941 to 1945, had developed several strains of hybrid corn and, with his writings, helped hybrid seeds become a commercial success.

The usual method for gathering corn was to drive the team over one row and pick two rows on either side as well as the row behind the wagon. Huskers threw the ear into the wagon as it was separated from its husk. The team—at voice command—moved on a little at a time. Cribs for storing the corn were built in the same manner as a cabin except they were made only five to eight feet wide and longer. Corn sometimes was slip-shucked *(picked with the husk on)*. Husking would be accomplished later at a husking bee. It frequently happened that deep snows prevented corn from being gathered at all. In that event, prairie chickens undertook the job, but they did slovenly work. After corn was gathered, cattle were generally turned into the field to eat up the husks and any blades left on the cornstalks.

Stems of wheat, and in the shock

The glory years for wheat growing in Linn County were from 1840 to 1852. During our first seven winters we experienced deep snows that afforded good protection for fall wheat. After the winter of 1845-46, a series of open winters, without protective snow, caused such failures for fall wheat that farmers abandoned it for spring wheat. Eventually wheat growing became a curiosity in Linn County. Mills went down and farmers bought flour from other states, especially Minnesota. Later wheat has been grown again with some fields yielding forty or fifty bushels to the acre.

One source reported that 175,655 acres of land were under cultivation in the county in 1874. The year following was the peak year for wheat. More than 52,000 acres were planted to spring wheat, nearly 92,000 to Indian corn, and nearly 23,000 acres to oats in 1875.

Fall wheat was generally grown in cornfields where standing cornstalks would hold the snow, and protect young plants from exposure to the wind. Wheat was sown about 1 September, or a little earlier, at the rate of one and one-half bushels an acre. Thicker sowing would have produced a better yield. This wheat was cultivated or plowed in with the big shovel plow. Sowing wheat in corn, especially in hot weather, was a hard, uncomfortable job any way you did it.

Soil that had been plowed in the fall frequently was sown to spring wheat. Sometimes cornstalks were cut off and burned, and wheat sown with no plowing, only harrowing. This practice resulted in weedy wheat fields. A yield of twenty to thirty bushels per acre was called a good crop. I never knew it to exceed that, except in one case when fall wheat was sown two bushels to the acre. There were many conditions and diseases that caused wheat to fall short of a good crop. Droughts or wet seasons could prevent planting in good time and good conditions. Diseases like rust, and insects like chinch bugs preyed upon it all. In addition prices were often ridiculously low. Wheat sometimes would bring only fifty cents a bushel. More than once it was as low as twenty-five cents. Such low prices after hauling it 50 miles to market were disappointing at best.

We did not have long to wait before enemies appeared in the wheat fields. Scab and rust appeared early in wheat culture and remain enemies. Scab caused sections of the grain head to die out before it matured. Wet weather was blamed for scab. The greatest and worst enemy was the chinch bug—a little wheat bedbug that cuddles down around the stems of wheat and sucks out the juices. As the wheat grows, the bugs gather around the joints and weaken the stem so it breaks down prematurely. When the bugs become so numerous that there is no more room for them, they spread over into the cornfields.

Early in the 1840s rust appeared on the wheat and continued off and on as long as wheat was grown. Then the existence of rust was attributed to excessive moisture followed by sudden spells of hot sunshine. Seldom, if ever, did farmers become seriously alarmed over the appearance of rust much before harvest time. Many sought to save their wheat by cutting it green before rust shriveled it. Damage from rust occurred mostly during the first 15 days in July. Scab, rust, and chinch bugs caused wheat to become unprofitable by 1880. Increasing profits that could be made from producing corn, hogs, cattle, and butter softened the loss of wheat as a crop.

Twenty-five to thirty years after wheat growing died out and started again in Iowa, we are told that the barberry bush is the demon causing ruinous rust. The government said the barberry *(a shrub characterized by spines, yellow flowers, and red berries)* was responsible for killing two hundred million bushels of U. S. wheat in 1916. It ordered extermination of the culprit bush. One barberry bush in a city yard may destroy hundreds of acres of grain within a short time because the fungus parasites settle on the bush's leaves in mid-May. Then they reproduce themselves each five days, spreading like wildfire on the wind. A notable fact about the barberry bush is that it was not native to Iowa nor any of its adjoining states. It was introduced by the hand of man.

The early nurseries of Linn County did not introduce the barberry bush before they were destroyed by the Grange and Jack Frost. On pain of boycott the Grange forbade nurseries to sell fruit trees at more than three cents apiece; Jack Frost killed orchard trees outright at the beginning of the 1870s. The great Mound Orchard began its decline at this time. The bush is native to New England states. Eastern agents who worked the country probably introduced the barberry bush.

George Greene owned Mound Orchard. After devoting more than ten years in the Fifties and Sixties to develop the orchard and grounds, he built his home there in 1867. Greene's orchard encompassed more than one thousand acres; an English gardener tended the grounds around the house. Every kind of tree and shrub that could be grown in Iowa was represented. Greene had bought the site from Joel Leverich; he rented the farm to Joseph Hollan and his wife Susannah (Lucore) from 1844 to about 1848. The Hollan home sheltered the first class of Methodists in that area while the Hollans were in residence (Arnold). Mount Mercy College acquired the site in 1928 (Murray, pp. 10-12).

After harvesting, wheat grains had to be separated from stalks

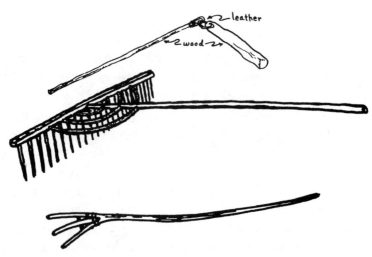

Tools for harvesting wheat: Flail (top), wooden rake and hay fork

13 Harvesting

Harvesting wheat with a cradle scythe

THE hand sickle reaped our first one or two wheat crops. The sickle was long and curved. The right hand thrust the sickle into standing grain while the left hand grasped the heads of the bunch to be cut off. Each bunch was laid on the stubble and as many more bunches added to it as was convenient. Swaths cut with the sickle were narrow.

In Pennsylvania where we had lived it was customary for reapers to go in gangs of fifty or more. Each gang had a 'puller' (leader) and a 'pusher' (driver) to keep the men at work. Pullers and pushers received extra pay. The puller would begin first and by the time he had reaped two or three feet another reaper would start in until all were engaged. The pusher, of course, went last. If any worker failed to keep up with the rate set by the puller, the whole line behind him was affected. The pusher then would push up on the one in front of him, compelling him to push the next one and so on, until all the laggers were prodded along.

As the puller finished his turn, he threw the sickle over his shoulder and hurried back, carrying several little bundles together to make a sheaf. Then he started reaping again; the others followed in their order. It was a type of endless chain in which there was no let up.

By the time people were prepared to raise big crops, the cradle had been invented and operations were revolutionized.

The cradle consisted of a scythe fastened to a framework of four supporting fingers. As the scythe cut and followed through, the grain fell back on the fingers that were nearly parallel with the ground. Then with a sudden jerk the grain was thrown off the fingers onto the stubble where it lay straight in a swath. The grain was later raked with a wooden rake and bound in bundles by hand, using a portion of the cut grain. A cradler cutting a swath eight or nine feet wide could cut two acres a day for which he was paid two dollars. A man who could rake, bind, and keep up also got two dollars a day. All others, except boys, got a dollar a day.

In about 1847, *the year McCormick began manufacturing his reaper in Chicago,* the reaper was introduced in Linn Grove. Four farmers together bought one of the machines. This method of reaping with horses and machine was a wonderful invention that immediately put the cradle to rest. The aggregate harvest of the four farmers amounted to about two hundred acres besides a little harvesting they did for others. Although conflict arose at times over the order of cutting, it never became serious but did suggest the advisability that three of the men sell out to the fourth.

With five or six binders and two shockers, we cut and put up ten to fifteen acres a day. Most of the grain was stacked in shocks and allowed to sweat before threshing. The threshing season lasted late into the winter. Threshing grain with a hickory club disappeared with the sickle. Tramping grain out with horses came into vogue with the cradle. A circular dirt floor—about twenty feet in diameter—was cleared. Around the outer edge of this floor, grain was unbound and positioned with heads uppermost in a tier four or five feet wide. One or two spans of horses were brought onto this bed of grain. A small boy rode each span or *team of two animals.*

Round and round they would go while the horses' hooves pounded the wheat out. Two men with forks, one on the outside and one on the inside of the tier, continually turned and stirred up the grain as it was being tramped. After the straw was raked off, another grain bed was laid down and the tramping repeated. The grain was then gathered up and run through a fanning mill. By this time, fanning mills had superseded the natural air for cleaning wheat. The first and only fanning mill we ever had was made in Cedar Rapids—probably in the early forties. Large yellow letters were inscribed on the drum: Higley & Baker, P. R. Lawrence, maker.

The horse treading process gave way to the chaffpiler, another wonderful invention—cleaner, more expeditious, less exposed to heavy rains. The chaffpiler was forerunner to the threshing machine. The uncovered cylinder with tumbling shaft was powered by four horses. One chaffpiler was owned by several Linn Grove farmers but—unlike the reaper—no special priority in use existed because threshing was not so limited by time and weather. Threshed grain was stored in pens built of common ten-foot fence rails with straw used to cover the floor and fill cracks between the rails. Sometimes several pens were joined. The ground for about twenty feet in front of the pens was cleaned off, and the cylinder set on the outer bounds of the floor. The force of threshing threw straw, chaff, and wheat all along the length of the floor to the pens. Men were stationed to rake off the straw.

When wheat and chaff were piled as high as convenient, the machine was stopped and all hands shoveled wheat and chaff into the pens. They covered it with straw, and awaited a convenient time for winnowing and marketing.

I do not think we had built granaries or bins for storing cleaned wheat to any extent before the winnowing threshing machines came into use. However, my father had cut down one of the famous bitter elms that grew in Linn Grove. The tree was about six feet in diameter. He used the hollow for storing grain. At the lower end it held ten bushels to the foot.

Forerunners to the Threshing Machine

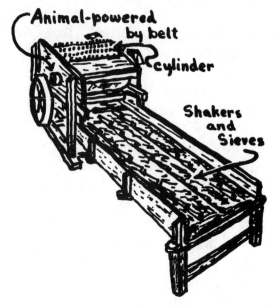

Animal-powered Thresher and Separator was patented in 1837

Man with a rake removed cut grain from 1847 McCormick Reaper

14   Two Types of Mill

Mills grind grists of grain or saw lumber

EASTERNERS were mistaken in their belief that Iowans ten or fifteen years after early settlement were still living on corn alone. After the first year, we had wheat bread as good and as plentiful as did our eastern cousins. Nor did we for long have to take wheat to Cascade for grinding. A mill was soon put up on Buffalo Creek, about three miles above Anamosa in Jones county. Called Pete's Mill, it was quite convenient for the people of Linn Grove. On one occasion I went with my father to this mill. A neighbor with a grist of his own went along. All went well on our way to the mill.

Coming home with the flour we began fording the Wapsipinicon River. As we got to the middle in the deepest water that came up nearly to the wagon box, Father's horses balked and would go no farther. After an impasse of several minutes, the last resort finally came. Our neighbor drove his team to shore, unhitched it, came back, took our team off, hitched his team on, and pulled our wagon to shore. Then he hitched our own team to the wagon again and we all continued homeward as though nothing unusual had happened.

Other mills were scattered about the country. McLeod's Mill was built on the little stream that flowed from the two big springs north of Cedar Rapids. A small mill, called Keith's Mill, was put up on Indian Creek near Kenwood. Later a good mill was put up on Otter Creek, and another on Big Creek that was known as Scott's Mill. By design the earlier mills were overshot mills. They turned the old-fashioned stone burr that made the good old-fashioned flour.

You might try to convince an old settler, who had tasted such flour, that modern patent flours are just as good. He wouldn't believe it. These mills ground corn, wheat, and buckwheat, but did not bolt *or refine the product.*

Old-time mills were called gristmills because they ground grain by grists, separately and solely—each lot for the man who brought it. It was generally understood that millers were not allowed to charge cash for grinding without consent of the grist owner. They took a portion as pay for grinding. This was according to a special law *passed by the territorial legislature in 1838-39 to regulate mills and millers. It was to protect people from being deprived of food if they could not pay cash* (Laws, pp. 343-346).

Besides regular gristmills, there was a small one called corn cracker for grinding corn only. The owner, *Jacob Mann,* said it was the spunkiest little mill he ever saw because as soon as it had ground one grain it jumped right at another. In the great freshet and flood of 1851 this mill with its owner aboard migrated down the creek and never returned.

John S. Oxley, with the assistance of Jacob Mann, had built the county's first gristmill on Big Creek in 1842-43. It was located in the extreme northwest corner of Linn township. In 1848 Mann bought the mill for $500, which he hoped to pay out of earnings. Mr. Mann had only a hazy idea of finance, but the mill was his life. There was no lack of grinding business and the mill operated at times both night and day. On 5 July 1851, there was high water in Big Creek and elsewhere. Sally Mann begged her father to close the mill during the night because the skies seemed to threaten dangerously.

Jakey's reply: "If the mill goes, I want to go with it."

During the night the center of a great storm passed through, raising the creek, it has been said, 20 feet in 20 minutes. At daybreak, the Oxley family peered

*across the river-like flood. Sally stood in the doorway
of her nearly engulfed cabin. Showing great grief she
shouted, "Pap's gone with the mill."*

*A search was begun and, several rods downstream,
Jakey's body and the door of the mill were found high
up on the creek bank* (Oxley, Mills). *Sarah 'Sally' Mann,
who had come to Iowa with her father and brothers,
was the first white woman to settle in Linn County* (1878
history, p. 335).

A number of sawmills were built along the creeks to
provide lumber for the settlers. One circular saw, powered by
horse, made its appearance in Linn Grove as early as 1844 or
1845. Its operator, William Morehouse, moved the saw rig
from place to place in the woods, and sawed lumber near
the source.

When big flouring mills were put up in Cedar
Rapids, they did not grind grists but rather exchanged flour,
shorts *(byproduct),* and bran for the farmers' wheat. They also
bought wheat outright. These mills generally gave from 30 to
34 pounds of flour and a specified portion of the shorts and
bran for a bushel of wheat. The bran part was not of much con-
sequence in those times when it sold for only three cents a
bushel instead of three cents a pound as it does in 1919. This
exchange was not always satisfactory to the farmer who
thought he did not get enough flour for his wheat.

*Foundations for the world's largest cereal mill were
made in 1873 (first by North Star Oatmeal and then American
Cereal). The Quaker Oats plant burned to the ground in
March 1905 and modern buildings of concrete replaced them.
American inventor Oliver Evans, of Wilmington, Delaware, had
built an automated factory in 1785; it was the forerunner
of all flour mills* (Smithsonian, p. 191).

15   Indian Neighbors

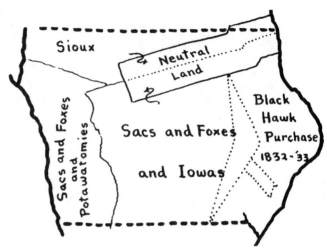

40-mile wide neutral zone keeps tribes apart

WHENEVER Indians came into our neighborhood they camped on the Hiram Thomas claim, almost three miles from us. It was near the cabin of my oldest brother, Lewis Kramer. Lewis' son was about three years younger than I, and William Andrew naturally became more familiar with the Indian language and ways. He and my brother Michael often went to their camp to wrestle, run races, and shoot arrows with the skinneways *(young males)*. The older Indians took great interest in these performances and showed disappointment when their own were outdone. Several instances of the family's contact with these *Native Americans* illustrate the good will that existed among them.

One day our nephew William, brother Michael, two sisters, and I were together in our cabin when several Indians came on a friendly call. William was well acquainted with them. They began to play, making fun, and playing tricks on each other. Then they got slate and pencil, each trying to make the best picture. The play continued all day, and at evening they quietly went home to their wickiups.

On another occasion old Mullinee, his squaw, and papooses called at our cabin. When they were ready to leave, we gave them some potatoes and fat pork—a treat to them. Mullinee took a long string of beads from his neck and, to express his appreciation, wrapped them around my sister's neck.

On the claim where we lived two cabins were joined. One was kept for storage. The cabins were situated on two acres enclosed by a brush fence. One cold morning before sunrise Father saw Nonaquatta near the gate looking at something on the snow. He asked what he was looking at.

Nonaquatta replied, "Buck track."

Because some sixty hogs had been running all over the place, Father argues, "It is kokkush track."

The Indian said in English: "I reckon I know."

Father then invited him to breakfast. After breakfast the Indian picked out his buck track from the hog tracks and followed it through the enclosure and beyond. About sundown as Father was going up the Grove he met Nonaquatta about half a mile from our house. He had a buck on his back. Father invited him to supper; he stored the buck in the spare cabin. His buckskin leggings, covered with three or four inches of ice, were a long time thawing. He hastened the thawing with his knife, scraping until all the water was forced out. His garment became soft and pliable again like newly tanned buckskin. When ready to leave, he went to the spare cabin and, with his knife, cuts off a hind quarter of the buck for Father. He said his squaw would come for the remainder of the deer in the morning. She and the papooses came and Father gave them potatoes and pork. They went on their way rejoicing.

Father bought a pair of moccasins from Mnasnes and, finding them very good, ordered a second pair. He paid for them in advance. About that time the Indians were removed to a reservation *in Kansas* before Mnasnes had delivered the moccasins. The Indians were dissatisfied with their new home and frequently visited their old hunting ground. Meeting Nonaquatta one day, Father asked if he knew anything about Mnasnes.

Pointing westward, he replied, "Away Massasepo nipo," which meant that he had gone beyond the Missouri River and died. Little wonder that he had not delivered the moccasins. We never doubted his honesty because we found the Indians far more trustworthy than many of the whites.

We have no knowledge that Indians ever stole anything from the whites, although whites made a business of trading with the Indians to cheat them. We suspected once that some bucks stole corn from our crib to feed their nackatuckasies *(ponies)* while the older Indians were at the cabin, but we had no positive proof. They did not seem such beggars in those days as they afterward became. Perhaps their new behavior was caused by contact with whites. In their earlier condition, they were on the whole an honest, peaceable, and friendly people who appreciated favors.

Those who roamed over Linn County when we came to Iowa were branches of the Sacs and Foxes who formerly lived in Michigan. Their language and habits were similar. Some Indians among us probably had been warriors in the Black Hawk War of 1832. Following that war, those in Iowa named themselves Mesquakies, which means friendly. They live in 1919 on the small settlement at Garwin in Tama county.

More than 150 Linn County residents in 1852 signed a resolution recommending, "the Indians should be permitted to remain in the country unmolested until they can petition the Governor for release, or that some action be taken in their behalf." Among the signers were Hiram Beales, William Broady, C. C. Cook, George Greene, Nathaniel McBride, and Hiram Thomas. Nearly 400 residents petitioned the U. S. Congress in the same year of 1852 requesting that the Mesquakies "be allowed to have . . . a residence within the State of Iowa on the unsold lands." The petition explained that many of the Indians had been removed by the government to 'unhealthy' lands where their children died off rapidly, and that they lacked sufficient force to sustain themselves against more powerful neighbors who surrounded them. Signers included C. L. Brockman, Isaac

Butler, Isaac Cook, L. (Lawton or Lowell?) Daniels, William
English, W. Granger, R. D. Stephens (Courtesy of Phil Morris from
papers found at the State Historical Society). *The Mesquakies bought*
80 acres along the Iowa river in 1856. By 1914 the 368 Tama
Indians owned 3,890 acres. The settlement was mostly made up
of Fox with a few Sac and Potawatomi Indians (Christensen, p. 84). *The Indians finally were granted citizenship in*
1924.

Moving about in gangs of eight to fifteen or more, the
roaming tribes stayed at a camping place a few days or
weeks. Other tribes also roved over portions of Iowa and
sometimes came into sharp conflict for trespassing on another tribe's hunting grounds. To avoid such trouble, the
United States government established neutral zones, 40 miles
wide, between the tribes. The tribes were forbidden to cross
for hunting purposes. This greatly reduced trouble between
the tribes, and the whites were not affected.

Only a small body of Indians hunted over Linn County.
It seems the government allowed them to hunt until the lands
were sold to individuals. Their tent cloth, if we may call it
cloth, was made of flag leaves tied together into mats with
thongs of deer sinew. The edge of each flag leaf was laid over
the edge of the preceding one and each leaf tied at the
ends and perhaps at the middle. The leaves fit so close they
were almost air tight. Perhaps most tents were cone-shaped
with a hole at the apex to let smoke escape. No more smoke
lingered in the tent, if as much, than was usual in the white
man's cabin. The Indians chose dry slippery elm for their
fires. It was the best wood to be found for making coals and
holding fire. They were successful in finding dry wood, and
when long pieces were available slipped one end under the tent
and pushed it along to make fire at the middle. When the center burned off, they shoved the pieces together to keep up the
fire. The Indian thought the white man's fire was too big for
getting close enough to keep warm. Although the fire was
small, it was sufficient. They carpeted and lined their tents

with fur, and it was warm and comfortable in the coldest weather.

When preparing to move, the Indians rolled up the covering into great bundles and swung them over the backs of ponies. In their frequent migrations, the Indians carried tents, furs, and all other fixtures and belongings on ponies. Squaws and papooses sat on top as they marched along in single file. Their ponies made their own living, except in the wintertime when squaws cut down linden trees that seemed to be the animals' principal food.

In the early days many people who knew nothing about the *Native Americans* or their relations with the settlers assumed that *newcomers* to Iowa would face certain death sooner or later. They also had misconceptions about the number who were supposed to live here, and of their bad deeds. The fact was that comparatively few were making a home here. It is true we saw Indians often, but they were nearly always the same little roving gang making its rounds, camping for a while and then moving on. The misconceptions led to misunderstandings that are best illustrated by what was called "the Plum Grove Battle." The following is the way I heard the story

Three miles west of Cedar Rapids two Indians were out hunting and one of them shot a prairie chicken. A white man heard the shot. Looking around, he spotted the two Indians with guns. Surmising they were shooting at him, he started to run. Fearing the white man might raise a false alarm, the Indians attempted to catch him and explain that they were only shooting at prairie chickens. Their pursuit frightened him all the more. He succeeded in outrunning them and raised the alarm. "Indians are coming, destroying everything, killing the people, and burning houses." Messengers were sent from Cedar Rapids to warn Marion residents of the impending danger.

People at Marion hastily gathered up teams of horses and ox wagons, and loaded up forty women and children. A little plum grove four miles east of Marion was supposed to provide safety. On arriving there they sent out scouts to locate the enemy. When silence and suspense could be endured no longer, the refugees spread out their search—back to Marion. It was peaceful and quiet there. Not one citizen seemed to know anything about the battle. A humorous historic report of the battle was duly recorded in the *Linn County Register*.

Since that newspaper was renamed the Marion Register *in 1864, the article Uncle Isaac refers to must have appeared sometime between 1852 and 1863. The 1878 history* (pp. 399-400) *and Christensen* (p. 84) *give the date of the ridiculous Indian scare as Spring 1847, and locate its origin near the town of Westport.*

Some basis for fear did exist. The first of two actual Indian atrocities occurred 25 March 1843 at the Tegarden cabin in northeastern Iowa. Two white men were sharing liquor with three members of the Winnebago tribe, and had previously engaged in sharp trading practices with their drinking companions. Other whites believed the two men deserved their fates, but the Indians also killed Tegarden's wife and three-year-old baby while they slept. A boy, 9, and girl, 7, escaped by playing dead. They later recovered from their wounds to tell the story (Brown, pp. 14-16).

The second incident took place 14 years later on 8 March 1857 in western Iowa. An outlaw band of Sioux, headed by the infamous Inkpaduta, killed more than forty innocent white settlers. It was called the Spirit Lake Massacre.

16   Outlaws and the Goudys

Hiding money at home was the practice

MONEY was scarce but those who had some devised various ways of hiding it. Few early settlers possessed more than a hundred dollars in money, and many had none at all. It was common practice to bore holes in the log wall for pins on which to hang clothing. One man, at least, conceived the idea of shoving his money into one of these holes before driving in the pin for his coat.

The Goudy robbery took place about the time Father was splitting rails to fence his little wheat field. The Goudys were not the robbers; they were the robbed. Three Goudy homes were close by one another in Linn Grove. They included the father and wife, *John and Sarah Goudy,* a son-in-law and daughter, *Thomas and Mary McElheny,* and two sons, *Captain Thomas Goudy and Samuel Goudy. The Goudys had come from Wayne county, Ohio in the summer of 1839 to settle on the claim made during a visit earlier that spring by John Goudy and a son. The Goudys bought a half-section of land (360 acres) for $600 from Mr. William Gilbert. Gilbert was probably a land agent for the government.*

When the robbers entered the senior Goudy's house that night in February 1840, some gang members stood guard over the beds with clubs. They ordered the occupants to keep their heads covered. One robber stood by the door holding a candle, and others searched for money. They turned everything in the bureau drawers upside down. If I remember rightly, they secured nearly a hundred dollars.

The gang next went a mile and a half to the home of William Gilbert at the upper part of the Grove. The robbers easily found all the man had in a secret drawer of a desk that he had bought that very day from my father.

How did the robbers know where the money was hidden and how to open the secret drawer? Mr. Gilbert's near-neighbor *(Goodrich)* was one of the thieves. He did not do the actual stealing. His part was to find out who had money and where the owners kept it. When Mr. Gilbert came to our house with a sled to claim his desk, he brought *Goodrich* along with not the slightest suspicion. It did not occur to Father or Mr. Gilbert to exercise caution. In the presence of this man, Father revealed the secret drawer. The upper part of the desk contained a bookshelf with partitions. The middle partition appeared to be an inch thick. Actually it was made of thin lumber, assembled and veneered to look like solid wood. The desk had two drawers below. By pulling out one of the drawers, a wire could be reached; it tripped to open the secret place. *Goodrich* had rightly judged that the money would be found there. Additional evidence of the neighbor's complicity with the thieves was provided by Mr. Goudy's daughter. Hannah had seen this man through an opening in her cover on the night of the robbery. He held a candle near the door to light the robbers' way.

A short while after the robbery, deep snow covered the ground. One cold morning a while later some of the settlers met near our house for an outdoor party. They brought the robbers with them. One observer reported that he never before had seen it rain blood. That is how they described lynching *(or flogging?)* in those days.

A different date and account of the Goudy robbery, along with additional details of the fate of the robbers, were told in the 1878 History of Linn County (pp. 369-377). *The report also adds information about overnight guest accommodations of that day.*

At the hour of 11 o'clock on the night of 14 April, the

doors of the Goudy cabin were forced open. The residents awoke to find themselves in the presence and power of five desperadoes. The cabin had only one room and a shed-kitchen at the side . . . Two beds were in the main room. One of these was occupied by Mr. Goudy and his wife, and the other by the son-in-law McElheny and his wife. One robber covered Mr. Goudy with his rifle while another stood guard over the McElhenys. A third stopped the clock. (No explanation was given why he stopped the clock. Perhaps the ticking made them nervous?)

Daughter Hannah, who later married Judge John Shane of Vinton, related some of the details to the writer. The man at Goudy's bed demanded his money, threatening that if its whereabouts was not revealed, they would kill the entire household. Mr. Goudy said he had but little, only $40 that he had saved to buy some hogs. They would find that in his vest pocket. They insisted that he had more, and demanded it. The old man protested. The leader of the gang (Wallace) then ordered the house searched. He directed the occupants of the beds to cover their heads at once to prevent the family from recognizing any of the intruders—especially Henry E. Switzer of Cedar county. Switzer had visited the Goudy house only a few days before under the pretext he wanted to borrow money with which to enter his land.

Boxes, barrels, trunks, drawers, and pockets were ransacked without success. At last a flour barrel was upset. Its contents scattered out on the floor along with a purse containing $120 that belonged to Hannah. She had saved it from the change given to her by her father from time to time. An old leather belt that Mr. Goudy had used to carry his money around his person was also found. Careful examination would have added a $100 bill, concealed within it, to the robbers' booty. Enraged at not finding the $9,000 they expected, the robbers cursed the family before leaving.

They next went into Captain Thomas Goudy's home,

but found nothing except some provisions. Three of them next went to the house of William F. Gilbert. On this night, three men were stopping overnight with the Gilberts. There was the Dubuque-Iowa City mail carrier and two other men. Like Goudy's house, the Gilbert's had one room. Mrs. Gilbert and the children occupied one bed; the two strangers were in the second. Mr. Gilbert and the mail carrier had beds on the floor in front of the fire.

Rallying to attempt a defense against the intruders, Gilbert and the mail carrier were knocked down. One of the thieves smashed the mail carrier's cheek bone with a blow from a club. They searched the house thoroughly, and found the $50 bill and $30 in change in a secret hiding place of the desk. During the robbery, Mr. Gilbert's little son rose up in his bed and recognized Goodrich, the neighbor who lived a half-mile away. Total booty for the night's work was $240.

Captain Goudy and others soon started in pursuit of a man named Wallace whom they believed to be implicated. Old man Goudy went to Constable J. W. Tallman and Colonel Prior Scott, mill owner, for advice and counsel. Colonel Scott went among the people and inaugurated measures for organizing a mutual protective association. Lawmen from Bellevue in Jackson county, experienced in dealing with robbers, traveled to Linn Grove to assist in organizing a protective association. The meeting was well attended by delegates from Cedar, Linn, and Jones counties, and a Citizens' Association was fully organized (Reid).

Wallace was captured and turned over to Captain Goudy and his party. Switzer was arrested, and both men were held for trial at Tipton in Cedar county at the October 1841 term of the district court. James Stoutenberg (alias James Case) was captured at Conlogue's, taken into the woods and severely flogged. He was never seen again and some believed he was tied to a stone raft and left to his fate in the Cedar River.

Conlogue was arrested as an accessory to the Goudy robbery. After he established an alibi at the preliminary examination, he was tried—by rules not recognized in courts of law—found guilty, and sentenced to be hanged. A motion was made to change the sentence to whipping. Each citizen observing was to give him five lashes on the bare back until he told the particulars of the robbery. During the whipping, Conlogue finally admitted complicity and said he had received $25 as his share. He named Wallace as the leader on that occasion, and said Switzer and a man named McBroom were also among the five participants.

Neighbor Goodrich was tried by the same 'court' as Conlogue; the sentence was carried out by a man from Iowa City. McBroom was arrested and similarly tried by the 'court in the brush,' and sentenced to be whipped. He was taken to Big Creek bottom near Scott's mill, stripped to the waist, tied to a small burr oak tree, and whipped severely. Both Goodrich and McBroom soon left the country. Goodrich was never seen or heard from.

McBroom was sighted later in a Mississippi river city, leading an honest life. He had accumulated a fortune.

During his exciting trial at Tipton, Switzer escaped on his horse. He went west to continue his lawless ways. When Judge Shane and his wife visited California in 1874, they learned that Switzer had a fortune estimated at $40,000, and that several of his children were following in his footsteps. The judge planned legal action to recover the stolen Goudy money. A civil suit had begun shortly after Switzer's arrest in 1840 (24 years earlier), and a judgment had been obtained against him. When the judge returned home and asked to examine the old records, he found they had disappeared. Switzer died at his home near Vallejo, California in 1877.

It may be that Isaac incorrectly interpreted the "bloody" lynching he thought took place in Linn Grove. Perhaps it was the beating described in the history book? Or perhaps "historians" sometimes rewrite history?

17   Clothing

Hand carder helped prepare wool for spinning

WOMEN devoted themselves to manufacturing essential needs. They were both the motive power and operators of factories. They produced the thread, yarn, and cloth and made clothing for their families. Many early settlers brought wool and flax spinning wheels, and looms for weaving. They began work soon after arriving.

After the first season, growing flax for home use became a part of farm work. When ripe, flax was pulled and tied in bundles like wheat. Then, as soon as practical, the seeds were threshed out and the stalks spread out evenly on the grass. The dew and rain—or hand sprinkling—alternating with bright sunshine caused the woody substance of the stem to rot. It bacame brittle and easily broke loose from the bark fiber. This was called rotting the flax.

Flax was then ready for breaking, swingling, and hackling. Breaking was accomplished by a wooden machine striking the stalks and breaking them to pieces. These small pieces, called shives, were knocked out from the fibers of the bark with a swingling knife made of wood and shaped like a sword. The flax was held over the top edge of the swingling board and struck repeatedly with the swingling knife. It was then hackled by repeatedly pulling it over sharp iron or steel teeth to comb out tangled lint and straighten the flax for spinning.

The wheel for spinning flax was small, and the spinner could sit down and turn it with the foot treadle. The spindle was arranged to take up the thread as it was twisted. A distaff called "rock" was placed above the spindle on which the fiber was drawn. The woman's fingers regulated the thickness of the material.

Wool was prepared in a different way. A larger spinning wheel was used. Wool had to be washed and carded before spinning. Hand cards were used at first. Gristmill operators soon installed carding machines to perform this service. The cards were made of curved wire called teeth—all turned one way and probably fastened to leather. The hand cards were attached to 12x6-inch stiff boards and handles affixed midway on the back. Wool was spread over the teeth. With a card in each hand, the spinner pulled them over each other in opposite directions to loosen the fiber of the wool. This maneuver was repeated to tear the wool apart. Then it was rolled between the backs of the cards into a loose neat roll, three times as thick as those made at the mills, but only a third as long.

For spinning wool, a band was used to turn the spindle on the larger wheel. One end of the roll was attached to a thread at the end of the spindle. A small wooden peg applied against a spoke of the wheel sent the spindle whirling. At the same time quick movement of the left hand let out a portion of the roll and it began to twist, using about 10 to 15 feet or more. Once turned, the spindle generally kept whirling. Yarn was reeled off the spindle into skeins, and wound into balls for knitting, or bobbed for weaving.

Weaving on hand looms required a separate room, but spinning could be done in one all-purpose room. Although it was heavy work, women did all the weaving. Every tenth family had a loom; some made a business of weaving for others. Cloth made for men's winter clothing was called jeans and was made of flax or cotton chain with woolen filling. It was coarse and heavy. The durable quality was not to be despised in those times.

The most objectionable feature to that kind of clothing was its color—invariably the dirty yellow of a Missouri butternut or the dingy Kentucky pale blue. Women had to do their own coloring and the most desirable colors were out of their reach. For summer wear a great deal of linen was used. It usually went without coloring.

Flax spinning wheel (left) was smaller than the spinning wheel for wool

18   First Schools

School seat was made of puncheon or split log

EDUCATION of their children commanded great interest for settlers who were influenced by the Puritan ethic. The established standard was lower than it is today. It was generally believed that learning the fundamentals was all the education that was needed. A necessary education consisted of being able to spell, read, write, and 'figure' in the four fundamental areas of arithmetic. Girls studying arithmetic? That was out of the question. Arithmetic was too complex for them to understand. When grammar was introduced later, it was regarded with suspicion as a waste of time.

A school was started by subscription when enough children could be gotten together. Parents paid about two dollars a 'scholar' for a term of three months. The teacher boarded around with the families, a certain time with each. Subscriptions generally totaled from thirty to forty dollars for the entire winter. Only three months of school each year was practicable. Farm work continued up to late November. It began again with sugar-making about 1 March. The 'ship of school' in those days was hard to steer because many shoals and quick sands were strewn in the way. There might be trouble among the scholars, between teacher and scholar, or between parents and teacher. When one or two men withdrew his children and subscription, the school often broke up.

Schoolhouses for about the first ten years were log cabins built of unhewed logs. Chinked and plastered with untempered mortar, they were about the size of ordinary cabins, 16-feet square including the thickness of two walls. A stove if available was installed in the middle of the room where all could get around it. On many a cold day the scholars huddled around the fire trying to get warm.

The desks at first were made of puncheon and arranged against the walls, but some days it was so cold that they could not be used. The seats were half-log puncheon with pins driven into auger holes for legs. They could be moved near the stove on cold days, returned to the desks on moderate days.

In the winter of 1840-41 I attended my first school at Linn Grove. We met in a spare cabin on the McCormick claim, near the middle of the south grove. Here for two winters I attended 'Our Cheerful Happy School.' Mr. *David* Richardson was our teacher. Primitive as this school was, we had a debating club. We thrashed out the great national and domestic questions of the day—and 'spoke pieces.' On one of these occasions I spoke my piece. It was about bears and lions that groan and fight, because it is in their nature to do so, but little children were not to imitate them or tear out each other's eyes. As a supposed appropriate costume, I wore a necklace of bear claws. The necklace was not a product of eastern Iowa.

During the second year at Christmastime, a demand was made on the teacher by the scholars for a treat. To meet their demand he brought to school a bushel of small rutabagas that proved to be good ones and were quite acceptable. The third winter of my schooling in Linn Grove we went to a cabin that was probably built for school purposes. It was at the edge of timber about a mile east of our claim, and a mile or two from the upper end of the Grove. We walked through heavy timber nearly all the way. It was on hilly ground with a sugar camp nearby. This school was considerably farther from our home than was the previous school.

Here again Mr. Richardson was our teacher, and school was conducted as usual. Teachers were unwilling to lose even one day, and parents were not willing to pay for a day on which no school was taught. Again the scholars demanded to be treated on Christmas Day if they went to school. Of course it fell on the teacher to treat them.

Aware of what was expected, the teacher had prepared himself with many little biscuits. They were cut with a thimble about half an inch in diameter. When the demand was made, he began doling out his little cakes. Suddenly one of the biggest boys grabbed Mr. Richardson. Other boys, waiting to assist, quickly took the teacher in charge. They hurried him out-of-doors, put him in a sugar trough, and sent him flying downhill, on a toboggan-like ride. They next took charge of a Miss Drum—generally called 'the old maid'—who was attending the school. They sent her downhill the same way. Then, tiring of their Christmas frolic, the scholars dispersed to their homes.

Teachers thereafter appeared as usual at the schoolhouse on Christmas morning, but refused to assemble for school. They locked up the house and charged for the day. Parents could not refuse to pay. The following year we had a new teacher. I think that year and for two years following (1843 to 1845) we had a Mr. Humphrey from Cedar county. He was a good teacher and for those times up-to-date. He gave new impetus to the school, making it popular and giving it a reputation that brought scholars from far and near. He taught reading, handwriting, and inspired new interest in creative writing. He required the bigger scholars to write compositions. That was a hard blow. However, they persevered and developed abilities beyond expectations.

I remember one Calvin Newman. *At 18 he was much perturbed.* He took for his subject, 'What man has done, man can do again.' He received the highest praise for his writing. *Two years later Calvin Newman entered 200 acres of land in section 20 of Brown township. Tennessee-born and without money, he worked by the month as a prairie breaker to obtain funds with which to improve his claim. By 1849, he had built* a log house and barn and married Mary A. Howard. He was lauded in the 1878 history of Linn County as a 'self-made man.' Newman was then keeping 200 head of cattle, 15 head of horses, and fattening about 200 hogs (Chapman, p. 655).

The last day of Mr. Humphrey's school was made memorable by an address delivered to a large audience by Mr. Robert Smith—or Smyth as he was afterward called. His address stirred my heart to seek after knowledge and to obtain an education. Because of untoward conditions, my ambition was never fulfilled. Though I cannot remember a word that was said on that occasion, the savor of it has followed me all my life. *Smyth came to America from Ireland at age 20, worked as a clerk in Bedford county, Pennsylvania for six years before traveling to Iowa Territory by stage, steamer and on foot in 1840. He engaged in real estate and banking, read the law, and was admitted to the bar in 1854.*

Following Mr. Humphrey were three other teachers: Mr. Joseph Kyle, Mr. Freelingheysen, and Mr. Hamilton Goudy. More than one small boy looked upon Mr. Freelingheysen with considerable awe and respect. It was whispered about that he was writing a book. Books were few in those days, and the writing of a new book must be something wonderful. I didn't know then, as I know now, that of the making of books there is no end.

A new log schoolhouse was built near the Davenport road. It was much farther north and west of the one we had been attending. Here under the teachership of Mr. Goudy we ended our public school life, but our desire to learn did not die there. My brother Michael and I spent evenings, mornings, and noons going through the unfinished grammar and arithmetic books while plowing corn. Many a close contest we had on certain points as to which of us was right whenever we differed. *Isaac worked on the Linn Grove farm with his father and brother for twelve years, from 1840 to 1852. He learned and practiced all the farming skills. He attended school only three months a year from 1840 to 1850, along with some night school sessions during those periods.*

Those who started to school in 1840-41 never got more

than halfway through the arithmetic and grammar in the ten years we were in school together. Custom was the chief cause for the lack of progress. Each school year all scholars were put back to the beginning of their books and kept together with the newer recruits. The teacher was not always to be blamed; it was impossible to do justice to all. The variety of books and the many required recitations made it so. Many times he spent most of the noon hour with the more advanced scholars. Sometimes he worked evenings as well. Most interest and time centered on spelling; reading came next. The spelling book, Webster's Elementary, was made to replace McGuffey's *First Reader*. *(William Holmes McGuffey, a teacher and college president in the 1800s, produced a series of readers and spelling books, the first appearing in 1836.)* Although prepared for young beginners, the spelling book was nearly as difficult to read as any common book. After the spelling book, we progressed to the *English Reader* selection of prose and poetry. It was in quite fine print. Both were printed in 1840 and I have them still.

Books were scarce among the earliest settlers. Besides the Bible, a hymn book, a prayer book, and a few leftover school books, it is possible many families had no books at all. A small Negro song book or a dream book was occasionally circulated among the young folk. Father had brought several books to Iowa. I remember Mackensie's *Five Thousand Receipts* book, a number of Analytical magazines that were bound in hog skin over thin sawed boards, Captain Riley's Narrative, and a few others whose names I do not recall. *(Colin Mackensie who died in 1821 wrote Five Thousand Receipts in all the Useful and Domestic Arts. It was published in Philadelphia in 1825 as a 'complete and universal practical library and operative cyclopedia'; a revised edition in 1829 had medical information and an index.)*

Until the 1843-44 school year many books were used in the schools. Probably no two families had the same kind except for spelling. Uniformity came with the introduction of McGuffey's Reader, *Ray's Arithmetic*, and Kirkham's grammar. *(Ray's Arithmetic was first published in 1844; it contained 'simple lessons for little learners on the inductive method of instruction.' Samuel Kirkham's English Grammar was in use from 1800 to 1870.)*

Much attention was paid to teaching writing (penmanship). There was no other pen than the goose quill for some years. It died hard, finally giving way to the steel pen. Scholars thought it quite an art to make a good quill pen, and perhaps it was. The schoolteacher had to make and mend the pens, including those belonging to the parents. Sarsaparilla berries were often used to make ink.

After we had been in Linn County a few years, *Pilgrim's Progress* made its way into our family and had much attraction for me. *John Bunyan (1628-1688) was an English writer and preacher; he wrote Pilgrim's Progress in 1675 while he was imprisoned for nonconformist preaching. It was his most celebrated work, and his writing style was praised for its simplicity, vigor, and concreteness.* A few other religious books followed. Then came the Sunday school books, but many of these did not meet my conception of what a religious book ought to be, and so I did not take them to heart.

By the 1850s Iowans were moved to organize a state teachers' association at Muscatine (10 May 1854). Its purpose was to promote the education interests of the state, improve the quality of teachers, and elevate the profession of teaching. The state then had 859 schools; 459 were constructed of logs. One-third of the 1,299 teachers (740 male, 559 female) were under 21 years of age. Monthly pay averaged $19.73 for men, $9.79 for women. Principal textbooks of the earlier times were Mitchell's Geography, Ray's Arithmetic, Willard's History, Webster's Dictionary, McGuffey's readers and spelling books (Hastie).

The first publication in newspaper form that came to my notice was *The Youth's Companion*. It was brought to school one day by one of the scholars. I did not have the opportunity to read it, if then I was capable of reading. Nevertheless, for many years now I have been an interested reader. Although I had but little youth then, at about 87 I enjoy its pages perhaps as much as the young do. *(The Youth's Companion was published in Boston as a weekly for 100 years, from 1827 to August 1927; then as a monthly from September 1927 until 1929.)*

The first Iowa newspaper that came to my attention was the Iowa City *Reporter*. It was probably in the middle forties that I read and reread that particular issue until it was worn out. A stanza of poetry so fixed itself in my mind that it is still fresh as ever

> Of all that ever lived
> in woodland, marsh, or bog,
> that creeps the earth or flies the sky,
> the funniest is the frog.
>
> The frog the scientificist
> of nature's handiwork;
> the frog that neither walks nor runs
> but goes it with a jerk.

Those were the days when hymns were lined out two lines at a time so that the whole congregation might sing along. Most did not have hymn books. A small item in the *Reporter* told about a minister who could not see well. In lining out the hymn that began, "The eastern sages are coming in with messages of grace," he read: "The eastern stages are coming in with sausages and grease." His pronouncement contained a prophecy of coming worldliness. The stages from Iowa soon went into eastern cities with pork sausages and grease. These shipments greatly modified our life and society. *This story illustrates the change that occurred when markets for Iowa produce first began opening up in the 1860s.*

19   Keeping in Touch

Early blacksmith tools include anvil, hammers and tongs

WE first got our mail at Bloomington, now Muscatine, about 50 miles from our home. We paid Uncle Sam twenty-five cents for each letter received. Rates depended on distance: six cents for 30 miles; twenty-five cents for 400 or more miles. Letters were never prepaid.

We had no envelopes; letters were generally written on foolscap that made four pages. Three of the pages could be written on. The fourth was left blank and when folded the address was written there. People did not know anything about stamps to be licked as we do in the 1900s. Letters were sealed with red wafers (melted wax).

Postage stamps were first issued in 1847; penny post cards in 1873. A first-class postage stamp cost two cents in 1885, then three cents from 1917 until 1919 when Congress dropped it back to two.

We did not go for the mail every day or even every week. Whenever anyone planned a trip to Muscatine, he was laden with requests from neighbors who provided money in advance for bringing back their mail or various articles. On one of these occasions, Uncle Sam delivered a letter without charge. It had no address. The postmaster concluded it might be for some of the Kramer family, and it reached its proper destination.

In the early forties, we at Linn Grove got our mail at Marion. *The first post office there was at the Luman Strong inn and tavern. Luman M. Strong was born in Vermont and came to Marion after living in Ohio for several years. He was appointed first postmaster 7 March 1840 by the postmaster-general serving under Democrat President Martin Van Buren. Addison Daniels (Whig) was appointed postmaster to succeed Strong on 11 May 1842 under President John Tyler.*

Later we got mail at Saint Julian. This post office was on the Mount Vernon and Marion road, midway between Mount Vernon and Big Creek. I think it was the middle forties when we began to get mail there. The Saint Julian post office *(from 1846 to 1858)* was kept at the farmhouse home of Mr. John Safley. His wife was postmaster *(appointed July 1847)*. She received a salary of about $25 a year. Saint Julian was never laid out as a town nor was it called a town. Besides the post office, it had a sawmill. Earlier it had a good blacksmith shop with an excellent small plow factory. To Saint Julian I made weekly trips for the mail, traveling barefoot across three miles of prairie with burnt-off tall grass as sharp as needles. My feet were hardened for such conditions. *(Isaac was 14 in 1846.)*

Other early postmasters in Linn County are recorded at the National Archives in Washington (M841, roll 38, vol. 128): *Robert Smyth at Franklin appointed 11 November 1842; Isaac Butler, Springville 19 August 1843; Samuel M. Brice, Center Point 25 October 1844; Abel E. Skinner, Otter Creek 25 October 1844; Joseph T. Fales, Ivanhoe 25 May 1845; Joseph Greene, Cedar Rapids 1846; unrecorded name, Mount Vernon 8 August 1853; Martin Floyd, Lisbon 22 December 1854.*

The postmaster general ordered that three mail routes be established. Concord coaches began operating weekly in 1842 between several Territory towns: Dubuque and Iowa City, Iowa City and Marion, Davenport and West Liberty. Records show that J. R. Rickey received a contract for the Iowa City to Marion route on 30 April 1842. G. W. Gray took over the route in 1846 (Dwelle, p. 92).

20 Religions

SOME areas of our county were settled by families who were not religious, but had similar characteristics or were related. However, predominant elements of the society showed a religious tendency. Religious sentiments in our neighborhood were represented by three denominations: Methodist, Presbyterian, and Baptist. All had preaching services in Linn Grove almost from the beginning of its settlement. Perhaps the Methodists were the most dominant in the county but, in the Grove, Presbyterians were most numerous, including several Goudy families, and some Scottish Covenantors who associated with their meetings.

Two families, the Kramers and the Brockmans, were the only regular Baptists in the Grove. The *Andrew* Brockmans lived west of Paralta. Our membership was with the Baptist church organized at Marion in 1843. This church was somewhat tainted with the predestination doctrine. However, it allowed its members to believe and act upon the doctrine of free grace. One hard-shell Baptist in the Grove gloried in proclaiming his uncompromising doctrine. Occasionally the Baptist minister at Marion came to hold meetings in the Grove.

Methodists did not have continuous or regular meetings. Few lived in the eastern part of the Grove; comparatively few were in the western part. Their preaching of the doctrine of free grace was in broad, antagonistic opposition to the doctrine of the decrees preached by Presbyterians. Their meetings were not so scholastic in manner nor were they as hidebound in formality.

This attitude suited the free air of Iowa settlers who found the Methodist appeal more direct. Methodist class meetings had a compelling helpfulness. Their regular annual camp meetings especially aroused the interest of a new, sparsely settled country. Held near a good spring of water and in a shady grove, camp meetings were great events long anticipated. People flocked to camp meetings from many miles around. Sometimes those who came great distances camped out. For those who lived at a moderate distance, it was considered recreation to attend. To one who listened, the doctrines of free grace and eternal torture seemed the principal theme of their preaching. Those doctrines are now much in the background.

Camp meetings originated in Kentucky about 1800, and spread through the country. They involved both an emotional religious experience and a woodsy setting. At first, the meetings were ecumenical and included Presbyterians, Baptists, and Methodists. Camp meeting time was between wheat harvest and corn-gathering. It was one of the few occasions when people assembled in large numbers. Words to a popular camp meeting song were
> *"Come hungry, come thirsty,*
> *come ragged, come bare,*
> *Come filthy, come lousy,*
> *come just as you are."*

A saying that had some credence in those days was: "The good people go to camp meetings Friday, backsliders Saturday, rowdies Saturday night, and gentleman and lady sinners Sunday. The camp meeting gradually transformed into a Chautauqua center where the chief purpose was not conversion, but improvement or education or both" (Norwood, pp. 158-163). *The first Chautauqua was organized in New York state in 1874 by two men active in the Sunday school movement. A Cedar Rapids man, Keith Vawter, conceived the idea of a Chautauqua circuit in 1904. He envisioned providing talent at reduced cost for a select group of towns.*

By 1907 he was prepared "to bring not only a rich and royal uniform program, but tents, seating, and the whole physical paraphernalia necessary for the delivery of a six-day Chautauqua . . . (Orchard, pp. 113, 132-133)." An early Chautauqua in Marion was held in May 1917. Chautauqua provided summer work for college students, and cultural entertainment with religious inspiration for families.

Although Methodist congregations surpassed all other denominations, their ministers were not so well educated. Mr. Rev. George B. Bowman appeared to this young listener to be far from an educated man himself. However, with great energy and boldness he pushed educational matters upon his people and lo! Cornell College sprang up. *Two other colleges followed: Coe in Cedar Rapids, sponsored by the Presbyterian church, and Western (in southwest Linn County) by the Church of the United Brethren in Christ. All three colleges were coeducational and accepted female students along with male. Western was founded as a manual labor college in 1857 with nearly 100 students on lands provided by Jacob Shuey, Adam Perry, and W. A. Wherry. The village of Western grew to 250, but the college was moved to Tama county at Toledo in 1881* (1878 History, p. 464; Chapman, p. 954).

Rev. Michael Hummer of Iowa City first conducted a Presbyterian service in Linn Grove on 28 November 1840. Later that year he helped form the Presbyterian Church of Linn Grove. In early 1841 that church had 21 members. They included seven Goudys and the son-in-law (whose wife had died the previous year), and "Andrew Cramer (Kramer) and wife." Meetings at first were held in the homes of Samuel Stewart and John Goudy. A log schoolhouse built in 1844 served as the sanctuary for 10 years (Johnson). *For a number of years (1843-1848) their minister was an elderly man, Rev. Salmon Cowles. He also preached at Scotch Grove in Jones county, but had regular stated times to preach in Linn Grove. He was an old-style Presbyterian preacher, exact and stiff in his ways. He was firm in preaching the decrees of foreordination. The Presbyterian church did not attain the convenience of free grace until many years later. After Cowles came Mr. Rev. J. S.* Fullerton, a comparatively young man who preached alternately at Marion and Linn Grove. On his days for preaching at the Grove, people brought picnic dinners to the schoolhouse. Two sermons were preached, sometimes quite short. Once when a tipsy member of the congregation complained about a short sermon, Rev. Fullerton replied, "I can preach more in fifteen minutes than you can practice all week." Mr. Fullerton was still preaching for the church when the Linn Grove church building was put up out on the prairie northeast of the Grove in 1855 (Johnson). *During Rev. Fullerton's ministry two new Presbyterian churches were formed out of the Linn Grove membership at Lisbon in 1854 and New Linden, a now-extinct village northeast of Springville, in 1857.*

The Goudy family established and conducted a Sunday school. Elderly men and heads of families took charge and were the teachers. They were of the farmer class with the education of farmers, but they resolutely and zealously went into this work. I am grateful for what they did for me. I also attended a Sunday school in the schoolhouse west of us that was started and kept up by the Methodists.

Lithograph shows Cornell College as it looked in 1865

21   Politics and Paradox

MILITARY training days were appropriate while we lived in Pennsylvania—only 50 years after the end of the Revolutionary War. Seeing men in their decorated uniforms, officers wearing high cockades of bright colors was a wonderful sight. I found the maneuverings of both horse and man irresistible. The political significance escaped me.

After coming to Iowa, no such sights were seen, nor did we have training days—except on one occasion that to me was disappointing. *Possibly the occasion was in 1846 when Thomas J. McKean was training his Linn County squad for service in the Mexican War.* Uniforms and grace of movement were missing. The "guns" men carried were cornstalks pulled up by the roots—no match for my small boys' brigade that could put a flock of geese to flight when we charged them with mullen stalks.

The two political parties had been called Whig and Tory, the latter being shorn of its revolutionary meaning. Again they were called Radicals and Conservatives, or Whigs and Democrats. Finally Republican and Democrat became the established names. A number of other parties have sprung up since. These were days of political transition, not only of party names but of political thought and positions.

At an early day I followed my father to the polls. A large man, "mighty fond of whiskey," attracted my attention. This man declared emphatically that he was a Democrat. He mentioned the name of one candidate, and added, "I know he is a chicken thief, but I will vote for him because he is a Democrat." On this election day I overheard bitter bickering as individuals charged each other with dishonesty, lying, and cheating. In politics it seems anything is all right to gain a point, score a victory. The young boy brought up to respect justice, right, and truth is likely to view politics as a rotten game.

Linn County's first two elections were held in Westport. Thirty-two voters elected two legislators for the Territory government that met in the fall of 1838 at Burlington; Linn was one of 16 counties represented in that legislature. At the county level, the first three commissioners (supervisors) were elected in August 1839. They were Luman M. Strong, "a potential factor in all Linn County affairs," Samuel C. Stewart "distinguished for his piety," and Peter McRoberts of Franklin township. (Samuel Durham made the remarks about Strong and Stewart years later at a public gathering of old settlers.) The supervisors divided the county into three election districts when they met in October 1839 at the William Abbe home. As voting places they designated Abbe's home in the "Sugar Grove Precinct," one at Marion, and the third was at the home of Michael Green in Otter Creek township, northwest of Marion township.

Durham said, "All of these first county officers, after seeing Iowa well-established, (went) to other newer countries, not waiting to reap the full fruits of their labors here." His friend, Strong, went to Wisconsin in 1848 where he read the law while teaming between Highland, Wisconsin, and Galena, Illinois. As a justice of peace in Iowa, Strong performed numerous marriage ceremonies, including that of Durham and his bride in the early forties. In Wisconsin Democrat Strong became a legislator and was elected judge in the predominently Republican county (Iowa) at Dodgeville. McRoberts had moved to Tama county.

Conditions in Iowa allowed me to separate myself from political bickering, but I was not without positive convictions concerning the great political questions of the day. When Freesoilism was preached, I could see neither beauty nor advantage in it. *Freesoilism pertained to the Free-Soil Party. It was founded in 1848 to oppose extending slavery into U. S. Territories, and admitting slave states into the Union.* I thought that equalizing property all around would have to be repeated every year or two until there would be no property to equalize. When the slavery question came to the fore, I had my own thoughts about what was right. I timidly suggested to an older person that it was the right of the United States government to buy the slaves and set them free. This idea was met by a positive declaration that the cost would be prohibitive, but I was not convinced. At that time, there were about four million slaves; the highest price paid for the best in the market was a thousand dollars. Four hundred dollars would be a fair average price, considering sickly ones, old men and women, and children too young to work. The entire cost would have been little more than a billion and a half dollars. It was, however, in the province of politics to bring on a war to settle the matter. At war's end, it was reported that the dollar cost to both sides was seven or eight billions plus another fifteen billion in property damage. Besides the cost in money and property, a million lives were lost. *The accepted casualty count in the 1990s is that just under six hundred thousand died during the four years of the Civil War.*

Iowa, and Linn County in particular, enthusiastically supported President Lincoln and the Civil War. Linn's quota was 1,391; the county furnished 1,829 men including 438 executives (Baker, p. 759). *When war broke out in 1861, Thomas J. McKean, a West Point graduate, said, "There's going to be some fighting, and I must have a hand in it." He resigned his job as county sheriff and, leaving a wife and three young children, volunteered as an army paymaster. He was made a brigadier general, and later commanded a division at Corinth, Mississippi on 4-5 October 1862* (McKean pension files; Boatner, p. 534).

22 Isaac's Adventure

THE nearest market for wheat was Muscatine (Blooming-ton). Horses or sometimes oxen pulled the wagons that hauled it. The roads were poor and teamsters had to pick their way in bad places. This was called "cutting around." When making great circles was no longer practical, two farmers made the trip and double-teamed in bad places. Difficulties along the way were not all overcome when these places were frozen up. Snows continually drifted and packed down until a road was formed on a bank of snow from which no loaded wagon could be successfully turned out and back in again.

Under adverse conditions, the trip to Muscatine took about four days with three nights out. No more than 35 bushels to the load was possible. Prices paid ranged from fifty cents to one dollar a bushel—generally considerably less than a dollar. For a 35-bushel load of wheat, the average price would be from fifteen to twenty-five dollars. Farmers carried feed for their teams, except hay. They tried to time their trips so as not to stay in Muscatine overnight. The lodging bill in Muscatine for man and team would be a dollar. Along the way, it would generally be only twenty-five cents.

My earliest experience in marketing wheat was in late November 1843. I was 11 years old and my brother Michael 13. With our prairie schooner well loaded with wheat, we set out for Catfish Mill, *established in 1836 near Dubuque,* some 65 miles distant. Our mission was to sell the wheat and, with the proceeds, outfit two of us in clothing and books for school that winter.

We did not get far the first day, and that night we

were caught in a rain, but the wheat was not damaged. It began freezing the next day, and all day long the wagon wheels filled up with frozen mud. It was slavish going. By nightfall as we came near the lead regions, it was extremely cold. In the distance we could see dense smoke from the smelters. The man with whom we put up tried to keep me from going on the third day, probably fearing I might freeze to death. I appeared weak and thin while my brother looked robust and hardy.

"Your brother can go on alone, sell the wheat, and make your purchases while you wait here in a good warm place," he reasoned.

His proposal did not find acceptance. My brother and I arrived at the mill that day and sold our wheat for twenty-seven cents a bushel, receiving a total of $10.10.

At dusk we pulled into Dubuque, put up our team, and got our supper before starting out to do our trading. Our fare in Dubuque cost a dollar—the usual price for a man and team overnight with two meals. Perhaps people realized that since boys are small it took two of us to equal a man, and this was in harmony with boys' wages.

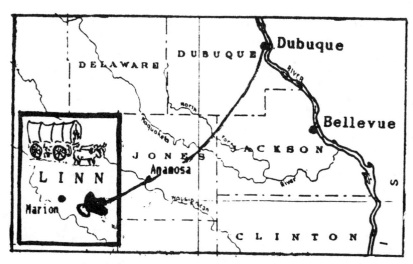

The route traveled by Isaac and his brother on their adventure

I had dug some ginseng that grew in considerable quantity in Linn Grove. We assumed no one but druggists would be interested. This lot seemed to have been put into an exposed corner of the schooner and got wet. As we made the rounds to the druggists, they would not buy it even though we explained how it got wet, and that it could be no more than an outside dampness.

After reserving enough money to pay our lodging expense, we had about $8.50 to spend. While we were trading for clothing and books at the dry goods store, the merchant overheard us talking about the ginseng.

"Do you have ginseng?" he asked.

"Yes," and I explained how we had tried and failed to sell it.

"The wetness doesn't hurt it one particle," he said after looking over the lot. He bought the ginseng at the regular price of twenty-five cents per pound, adding two or three dollars to our purchasing power.

Late in the afternoon of the fifth day we arrived back in Linn Grove after our 130-mile trek. We were happy and totally delighted with our achievement. We were outfitted and ready for the new school term, and eagerly looked forward to it.

23   Livestock

Hogs produced income; cattle provided milk and motive power

L IVESTOCK on the first settlers' farms included hogs, cattle, horses, and sheep in conjunction with wheat farming. Hogs were most valuable as income producers. Because most people were poor, they worked their way slowly into hog raising. Along with the other livestock, hogs were allowed to run at large over the prairies and through the woods. Hogs naturally took to the hazel patches and timber where they found most to live on: nuts, acorns, and various roots. With such liberty, hogs wandered far from home, sometimes several miles away. Different owners' hogs often mixed together, making considerable trouble. Many hogs became quite wild, and rounding them up was no easy task.

To identify his stock, each owner registered his own mark at the county seat *(Marion from 1840 to 1925)*. These marks consisted of slits, clips, or holes in the ears—either right, left, or both—in great variation.

Pork raisers in 1919 make as much pork in six months as we used to make out of running slab-siders for two years. Our slab-sided creatures could slip through the cracks of rail fences like eels. They were not slow to invade a place where corn or any good edibles were stored. Chinking holes to keep hogs out of stored corn was quite a business with the small boy tribe. It occurred to me that it would be more profitable and less vexatious to keep hogs penned up. The idea of hogs existing for a year without apparent cost had stronger appeal for grown-up boys.

Every fall after a general roundup, hogs were sorted and divided out to each owner. Hogs old enough were put in pens to be fattened for market. It took about as much corn to start the fat as it would have taken to summer the hogs had they been in a fat condition. This roundup, sorting, and putting in pens was no special delight to the small boy—nor to the big boy, either—if he would confess it. Farmers aimed to have their hogs fattened by the time hard freezing weather came.

Marketing was accomplished in one of three ways. The most common practice was to kill and dress the meat, and haul it on wagons or sleds. The markets were at Muscatine, Davenport, and Dubuque. This method had its drawbacks. Settlers often butchered in moderate weather and expected it to turn cold the next day. When it turned warm instead several days intervened before the meat was brought to market. Buyers were afraid the meat might spoil before they could get it to Saint Louis for processing. Sometimes farmers waited for weeks until the weather was safe for butchering.

Butchering a hog in mild weather was risky business

A second marketing method was for several farmers to join a drive, marching their porkers off afoot. This was quite satisfactory for the slab-siders that where accustomed to travel. Hogs too lazy to walk were given a ride to market.

A third method of marketing prevailed later on. Agents or buyers were sent out every fall to buy up hogs. They bought them in the pens at a certain price for the lot without weighing. The hogs were to be delivered on a stated day and to a specified place in the neighborhood. It took much haggling to drive these bargains. Delivering the hogs to a central pen was not always a comfortable job. The idea of a high wagon box fitted up against a suitable platform from which to drive hogs had not yet germinated. In those days dressed pork brought from $1.25 to $3 per hundred pounds. However, corn sold between ten and twenty cents per bushel. When dressed pork brought four dollars it was considered a fabulous price.

Horses were raised by the settlers but their production was slow. It was a long time before breeders were able to provide more than the basic needs of the country. Fifty or sixty dollars was considered a fair price for a good farm horse. Cattle in earlier days were raised almost exclusively for brood and milk cows, and for oxen. Little beef was eaten. No shipping business had been established to take them to market. Wheat growing decreased as cattle growing increased. Cattle for butter making and for beef became more profitable than wheat raising had been.

Sheep were raised almost exclusively for their wool. Seldom were any killed for meat. Wool was a necessity for making clothing then in use. Nearly every settler kept from 20 to 30 sheep. Any family without its own wool was at a disadvantage. Nearly all clothing worn in those days was made from wool and flax, spun and woven by the womenfolk.

A. J. Twogood, Marion's leading drover, drove cattle to Chicago

24   Sugar Camp and a Meteor

The auger bored holes for many uses

MAKING maple sugar was an early spring activity—a diversion shared by a large portion of the settlers before the farm work began. It was remarkable how clusters of maple trees were located throughout the groves to meet the needs of the early settlers so well. The clusters contained up to 300 trees and made practical the collecting of sugar water for boiling at one central place. Such a collection point was called "sugar bush" by Easterners. Westerners generally used the term "sugar camp," and applied it to the collection of trees, or to the building put up for shelter during sugar making, or merely to the boiling place.

Early in the spring sugar water runs out of the maple tree wherever it is punctured. Trees were tapped by boring half-inch auger holes and driving spiles *(spigots)* into the holes. Spiles from the pithy growth of the elderberry bush or sumac were cut in lengths of about one foot without joints. They become hollow tubes when the pith is pushed out. For the greater length of the spile, half the wood was cut away leaving it like an open trough. The water ran from the tree down to the end of the spile, and dripped into a vessel below.

The only vessel used in those early days for catching the water was the sugar trough. Made from logs a foot or more in diameter and three feet in length, they were split lengthwise into two equal pieces. The wood was chiseled from the inside, leaving a shell of at least an inch next to the bark, and two or three inches on the ends. The vessels were propped up level at the base of the tree beneath the spiles and might hold as much as two gallons apiece.

These procedures—tapping and driving spiles—were called "opening the camp." Gathering and storing the water followed. The weather regulated the flow, and the troughs must not be allowed to run over. That would waste the water. In times of excessive runs, it was almost impossible to take care of it all. We used a lizard *(conveyance)* pulled by a horse to gather the sugar water. The lizard was part of a tree trunk with two branches on which a platform was built and a barrel attached. We poured water from the troughs into the barrel, and dragged it to the camp where it was emptied into monstrous troughs, barrels, kettles, or any suitable receptacle. Meanwhile the boiling was started in great cast-iron kettles hung by big bales on poles suspended high enough to allow a fire to be kindled below. Fuel to keep the kettles going was all about us, gathered wherever we could get the best and get it easiest. To process all the sugar water, it was necessary to keep the kettles boiling day and night. For convenience, a camp building was put up and furnished with bedding so that two small boys might take turns in sleeping and in firing during the night.

When boiled down—still watery and not thickened like molasses—the syrup was taken off the fire and strained through a cloth. Then it was returned to the fire, and beaten eggs poured into it so that all impurities would rise to the surface for skimming. When a little of the hot syrup dropped in cold water would thread and break like glass, the batch was ready to be taken off the fire. If cake sugar was wanted, the syrup was poured into molds at once. For crumb sugar, the syrup was stirred continually with a wooden paddle until the moisture dried out and the sugar crumbled up fine. The amount of heat retained in the thick iron kettle facilitated this operation. This finishing process of making sugar is called stirring off. Batches of the strained syrup could be stored and kept for stirring off later. Campers sometimes arranged to visit one another on such occasions, and outside visitors came if they found out when a stirring off was at hand. To limit the demands of visitors, a rule was made: anyone who took a drink of water was counted out of the game and could have no more sugar. This helped restrict depletion.

Although old time sugar-making had its pleasures, it meant hard work—and exposure. Trees were tapped at the beginning of spring thaw and snow was still on the ground. Snow in the woods was often considerably more than a foot deep, and made chores more difficult. Wading about through this deep snow—to tap the trees, gather the water and wood, sled both to the boiling place, chop the wood, tend the fire, handle the water, lift off and on the heavy kettles, and all else connected with the process—did not make it an enviable job. Farmers today *(1919)* would say, "It doesn't pay."

Late in the season when the water began to spur around the edges of the troughs and the sugar would no longer "grain" well, we made molasses of it. A barrel of sugar water made from five to eight pounds of molasses—about two pounds to the tree. At the very last we boiled three barrels down into one, making "sugar water beer."

In the late 1840s while we were putting up a new sugar camp, there suddenly occurred a great crackling noise. It sounded as if muskets were being fired simultaneously followed by larger and sharper sounds, and a longer rumble. My brother was up on the building notching a corner. The noise and rumbling repeated several times. The earth and trees and the building shook so that my brother could not stand up. Squirrels came running out of their tree holes. We later learned this commotion was caused by the falling of a meteor fragment toward Iowa City. It was reported to have been five or six feet in diameter and to have sunk six feet into the ground.

The meteorite that fell about three in the afternoon of 25 February 1847 was called the "Marion Meteorite" because it fell nine miles south of that town. It was the first of five meteorites that fell in Iowa. This one broke into several pieces that ranged from two to forty-six pounds (Hastie, pp. 284-285).

A 21.4-pound fragment is displayed at Old Capitol on the University of Iowa campus in Iowa City.

A news story in the Iowa City Standard (28 April 1847) said one piece of the meteorite was found by Mr. Israel Mitchell. It had fallen about one and one-half miles west of the farm of Esquire Henry Rogers (in section 20, Putnam township, range 6). The writer speculated that it had fallen in February because "loud reports were heard by many of our citizens, and the conjecture then was that there had been a meteoric explosion."

One season some Indians rented timberland in the lower end of the Grove. It was owned by Mr. Thomas Goudy and had a sugar camp on it. Since it was several miles from his home and difficult for him to tend, he rented it, asking only that renters should tap the trees with auger and spiles. Boring holes with an auger was not in line with Indian habits. They bargained with him and gave him furs in payment for the damage to the trees that would result from their own method of tapping. With a hatchet they hacked into the tree giving the cut an upward slant, and drove the end of thin pieces of wood cut to the right length, into the cut. When the wood piece was dampened all the water would run down to the end and drop into the trough below. They made neat little troughs of elm bark, the only kind that peeled so early. They limbered the rough bark ends by shaving, then turned the ends upward and tied them tight with deer thongs.

After they opened the camp, Mr. Goudy went down occasionally to see that all was going right. On one visit a squaw brought him a ball of sugar. It was extremely hard and he noticed marks of teeth where the skinneways had been trying to eat it, leaving streaks of blood. For a moment he puzzled, wondering what to do with the gift without offending them—or eating it himself. His wits came to his aid. He told them that he would take it home for his own skinneway. That pleased them and as soon as he was safely away from them, his dog became the recipient of the sweet morsel.

25   Entertainment

The bob sled was a multi-purpose conveyance in winter snow

EVENING meetings at school were at first probably for the debating club. Some parents took part, commending the performances and encouraging the children to persevere. Still, debating was not regularly kept up like the spelling school that became the most popular entertainment of the time. At spelling school the selection of captains, their helpers, and a pronouncer was always interesting to watch. Seats were arranged on opposite sides. Captains chose their principals or best spellers. Each took a seat on his side in the order chosen, followed by alternate choosing of the remaining scholars.

When all was ready, the pronouncer gave a word to be spelled. If it was not spelled correctly, the contestant on the opposite side took a turn. Contestants on each side alternately took a turn until the word was spelled correctly. When the correct speller was on the side where the contest started, the game was called saved. If the opposing side spelled the word, it was charged as lost.

All spellers stood for the close of an entertainment. When a speller missed a word, he or she had to sit down. Sometimes a hard word would mow down both sides pretty fast. All but one speller on one team might be spelled down, leaving several on the other side. In this case each took a turn in spelling against that one person. Great effort would be made to find words that might cause the remaining one to misspell. For this purpose, words were selected from dictionaries, newspapers, and books—especially a word pronounced the same but spelled differently. For instance, the words "write." See that you write rite right, but when you write it as a man's name be sure that you write Wright right. If too hurried, this might confuse, but a good speller was well poised and not easily trapped. Sometimes the school had to close without getting him or her down. In spelling girls were as good as boys. *At least!*

After the close of spelling school, and other evening gatherings, there was a lively volunteer business. Boys volunteered to see the girls safely home. Though brothers and sisters often came together they did not always go home together. There was a great possibility of trading sisters. If there were no opportunities for an even trade, some of the boys were left to find their way home alone.

Night singing schools were also a part of the entertainments. Subscriptions were a dollar per scholar for 13 weeks. Sometimes older people subscribed a dollar to get the school made up. There were plenty of slackers. Some young men would not subscribe, but escorted their girls and enjoyed looking on. The slackers were not welcomed by either teacher or scholars, and in time were excluded.

Chanting geography and multiplication tables were other activities that brought forth night schools. In conducting geography school, the teacher hung large maps on the wall. These maps outlined but did not name all features necessary for a good understanding of geography. We soon learned to name by sight of location the countries and their kind of government, states and their capitals, rivers, seas, bays, straits, lakes, inlets, promontories, capes, and isthmuses.

With a long stick the teacher pointed on the map so all could see. He chanted each name twice before proceeding to the next, chanting it twice. When giving the name of a country, he moved his pointer all over that country. He did the same with rivers and bodies of water. He held the pointer still on towns while chanting their names, and so on. This system of teaching went the way of night schools. The 26 night lessons that I took made a more lasting impression on my mind than 100 or more lessons of regular recitations in day school.

Other diversions to school life consisted of plays and activities that remain common to school children in the early 1900s. Girls jumped rope; boys played baseball. Among the games for boys was a running game (like the hare and hound race), jumping, wrestling, throwing, and trials of strength. All were frequently practiced. Although the games were spirited, I kept aloof from them all except that I indulged a little in pitching "quoits." *Quoits is similar to throwing horseshoes.*

Other young men found great diversion and recreation in taking a gun out hunting, but I found nothing in it but drudgery and discomfort. I much preferred to plow in the field or hoe in the garden. Hoeing was about as great a recreation as I could find.

Freeman Smith (born about 1798) had been Isaac's first school teacher in Pennsylvania. He moved to Linn County in 1843 and gave 11-year-old Isaac a collection of seeds that encouraged his early interest in flowers. The gift led him to his life's work as seedsman and florist.

School "exhibitions" were prominent, and required the "learning of pieces to speak," both in prose and in poetry. Of course there were some great speeches to be "spoke" on the stage before the visiting public. These were not commencement seasons as we now have. They were the finishing seasons for ending the year's schoolwork. Little or no thought of school matters followed because each scholar knew that when school convened next year, all would enter the same grade. The "exhibition" at the close of school was intensely exciting and of great interest to those engaged in it. Perhaps it possessed the good qualities—inciting encouragement and good will—that the modern commencement possesses.

Although it was not part of our public school, the public swing was an important recreation for young people. Such a swing was located on the grounds now occupied by the Linn Grove cemetery near the Davenport road. (*The cemetery land was donated to the church by John Kyle in 1854.*) The swing was hung from a high limb of an oak tree. Made from the split butt end of a good sized sapling, this swing was high enough from the ground for two persons to stand up on. There was a crosspiece at the bottom with two split and trimmed side pieces to hold onto. The top end was trimmed to bend over the limb and was fastened together below the limb. This allowed it free play to swing back and forth. Two persons, alternately throwing their weight on it, could swing up to a level that looked quite dangerous. No accidents befell us. Young people met at the swing for jolly times in our carefree lives.

Pleasure rides were few and far between, and such excursions might be taken on horseback. It was quite common for women to have sidesaddles. When my sister Mary was married in the early spring of 1842, sixteen young couples rode 9 miles from Marion to Linn Grove to attend her wedding at her father's home. She was married to Mr. Edwin L. Hayes *by Rev. John Stocker.* After the ceremony the couples returned on horseback to Marion. Such a wedding party would be a novel sight in 1919!

Vehicles for the sole purpose of travel or for pleasure riding were not considered. In the wintertime we had our lizards, log boats, and long sleds for necessary uses. The long sled *(sometimes called a bob sled)* was fitted up with a common wagon box. It served for business purposes, visiting, and pleasure rides. Finally the sleigh was used strictly for travel and pleasurable purposes. Some sleighs had very high backs that sometimes sailed with the wind and, at other times, pulled against forward movement. The sleigh underwent vast improvements and many euphoneously named varieties came into use such as cutters, jumpers, skippers, flyers, and pungs.

One variety of sliding vehicle that I never found a name for was made of a log about four feet long and fitted with two small saplings that answered for sleigh runners. Auger holes and wood pins held it together. The slim ends of the two sapling runners were hewed down in front to serve as shafts. With a crosspiece and singletree attached, it was ready for hitching. I now call the vehicle the Katydid because it most resembled that creature and a "Katie" did ride on it.

One day a shy young lady bantered with the shy young gentleman *(Isaac himself)* to give her a ride. Of course he could not refuse. He seated himself astride the log with his feet braced on the crosspiece. She sat up sideways on the log behind him and held tight to him to keep from falling off, of course. They took their trip around the country for the pleasure of riding without saying a word to each other.

Such is the story as remembered and told to the writer many years later by Katie who rode on the sapling sled.

Although shy with girls in his younger days, at the age of 28 in 1861 Isaac would marry a young Irish lass whose name was not Katie!

Steer calves in training to pull sled will be oxen when mature at 4 years

26   Social Gatherings

Dancing to a fiddle replaced simpler country pleasures

OUR first social gatherings evolved around nut-cracking. Hickory nuts (or shell barks as we called them) and hazel nuts abounded in our neighborhood. Walnuts and butternuts were prominent in other locales. Going nutting was my chief delight and recreation as a small boy. My brother and I sought opportunities for gathering nuts and some seasons succeeded in gathering six or seven bushels. Then nobody thought of selling them. There was no market for nuts. What could be more natural than inviting guests to eat them? By force of circumstances, nut-cracking had to follow.

As small as our cabins were, they furnished room enough for living, sleeping, cooking, storing away spinning wheels, and entertaining visitors at parties. Hammers and stones were used for cracking. The cracked nuts were distributed around the party or set on the table in any kind of a dish that would hold them. Everyone helped themselves—picking out and eating the kernels. When shells fell to the floor we could tread them underfoot. No worry either when nutmeats got mashed on the floor. The big splinter on the puncheon had been roughed off with an axe, but that did not make the floor so smooth that one might be in danger of slipping. There was such freedom and liberty that everyone present could enjoy the party without fear or anxiety lest fine furniture or flooring be injured. There the old adage "blessed by nothing" prevailed.

Not the least of the social entertainments was the

husking bee festival. When planning a bee, the farmer pulled corn off the stalks, husks and all, and hauled it to a suitable place. He piled it on the ground in a long row four or five feet high at the center. When the corn was ready, a messenger on horseback scoured the countryside, inviting everybody to come on a designated evening. The pile of corn was divided into two equal parts by laying a rail on it at the center. Captains, who chose their huskers alternately, took their places next to the rail. Husked ears were thrown over and beyond the heap. The race became more exciting as it progressed. Sometimes the young women interrupted their kitchen work to boost the contest. At the finish, great hurrahing erupted as the victorious captain was carried about on the shoulders of his team. A big feast followed.

Lest you imagine the bee was an easy way to get corn husked without cost to the owner, you must realize that many ears were thrown over without husking. They might escape detection under the closest watching. Add the labor and cost of getting up the feast, and you see the profit must have been in party enjoyment.

Another kind of entertainment especially for young folks was called "The Party." The young engaged in games and all kinds of fun such as plays, witticisms, jokes, and tricks. Among the plays were "Green grows the rushes," "There was a young man sat down to sleep so early in the morning," "Open the gates as high as the sky and let King George and his men pass by." Forfeitures were acted out in a "pond." *Although no explanation for the "pond" is offered, it might refer to a designated area where kissing or performance of some other penalty took place for all to enjoy.*

Entertainments of this nature are now extinct; in 1919 the dance is taking its place. *At least one public dance occurred in Cedar Rapids as early as 1849, according to Dr. Carpenter*

On the Fourth of July a grand ball was given at the Coffman Hotel. Young people from Marion and all the surrounding country flocked to it. There were at least 50 couples. Beds were removed from our common sleeping quarters. Decorated with green boughs, it became a ballroom. Every part of the house was crowded and the fun was fast and furious.

Only one mishap slightly marred the festivities. Near a stovepipe hole at one end of the room the floor was defective. A husky reveler of more than ordinary weight, while executing the double shuffle, broke through and fell upon the heads below. No injury was done and the dance went on (Brewer Vol. I, p. 155).

Samuel W. Durham, 1817-1919

Thomas J. McKean, 1810-70

Luman M. Strong
1803-1867 >

REPRESENTATIVES at the First Iowa Constitutional Convention: Durham, a surveyor; McKean, a West Point graduate, and Strong, a county supervisor. Statehood was not achieved until two years later, in 1846.

Steamboats plied the Cedar River for 40 years

DISCOVERY of gold in California triggered migration from Linn County and elsewhere in the following two years (1848 and 1849). The excitement was so great that some of the best farms were sold for an outfit to take the adventurers west over the mountains. The trains of gold seekers all aimed to get across Iowa before the ground thawed in the spring and roads became impassable. However, many were caught by the thaw. Their departures were delayed until the ground thawed completely and the roads dried up. The stranded were in danger of not getting through before winter came again. Those from farther east who reached the plains before the thaw had good traveling. They got through in good season. Among those who left for the gold mines were Mr. Smith's son, Freeman Smith, Jr., *and also William Abbe, Dr. S. H. Tryon, Hiram Beales, Justice Wells, A. B. Dumont, Hubbard Shedd, Harvey and Henry Higley, Herman Boye, Dr. E. L. Mansfield, John M. Bardwell, Robert Ellis, J. F. Charles, and C. H. Harvey.*

During his western adventure, Smith discovered that 13 Freeman Smiths got their mail at the San Francisco post office. Freeman went digging for gold and succeeded in getting enough to carry him home again with a thousand dollars left for starting a pottery. His kiln was located in northeast

Cedar Rapids, above First Avenue, about A or B avenue between First and Second streets. His business was a failure because the clay contained some kind of material that swelled and burst when heated. He tried clay from several places around Cedar Rapids but found none suitable. Some clay from Mount Vernon showed promise, but hauling by team so far was too costly. Consequently his pottery went down.

In an early day, according to Mr. Doty, his father started a pottery in Westport, but it did not become extensively known. *The father, James Doty, who came from Ohio to Westport in 1839, started a pottery there in 1840 but died at age 38 on 17 January 1847* (Brewer, p. 482; Clarke, p. 145). Some years afterward a man named Spangler started a pottery at Mount Vernon. He seemed to be making quite a success of it, but death overtook him and there was no successor to carry on. *The 1860 federal census included John Spangler, 41, and gave his occupation as potter. Both he and his wife came from Ohio; they had two daughters.*

Censuses provide much information. Freeman Smith, Jr. was living with his parents and six brothers and sisters, according to the 1850 census. At age 26 his occupation was cooper, a maker and mender of barrels. When information for the 1860 census was gathered, Hiram Beales, his wife, and three children were living on their farm in Marion township. At age 51 Beales owned real estate valued at $3,750 and personal property totaling $4,000 in value.

Two or three years after Freeman Smith, the father, bought my father's Linn Grove claim he sold it to Mr. *J. S.* Varner, an ex-river pilot. Smith then bought a claim on Simons Creek near Paralta. A few years later, Smith bought the farm on which Oak Hill Cemetery in northeast Cedar Rapids is located. After moving to Cedar Rapids, Smith's company contracted to build a steamboat for service between Cedar Rapids and Waterloo. It did not continue long and probably was sold to go to other waters. I think two other boats were built at Cedar Rapids about that time for service to the South, perhaps down to Saint Louis. These boats also soon discontinued service; they were sent to other waters.

More than 750 steamboats were plying the "western" rivers by 1855. The first steamer to travel to the city limits of Cedar Rapids came in August 1844. She was the "Maid of Iowa" and it is said that rats first came to Cedar Rapids with this boat's cargo. The "Uncle Tobey" left in the spring of 1853 with a large cargo of grain and produce. Two other boats were built specially for travel on the Cedar. The steamboat "Cedar Rapids" was launched in June and left Pittsburgh on 1 July 1858. It arrived in Cedar Rapids three weeks later with 300 tons of freight and 84 passengers. George Greene was among the stockholders. During the next 14 months, the ship made twelve trips to Saint Louis. During its second season, the "Cedar Rapids" ran into and sank another steamer near Burlington. Long litigation caused the stockholders to lose their steamer. The timely arrival of the railroad provided alternative transportation. It arrived in Cedar Rapids in mid-June of 1859. The railroad was an idea improved on in America. The steamboat had been an American invention.

Early in 1858, a builder from Pennsylvania constructed a sternwheeler, the "Export," for Freeman Smith & Company, using wood harvested in the Bever Park area of Cedar Rapids. The "Export" made its trial trip to Waterloo in September with Freeman Smith, Jr. as master. During the winter, the company sold the ship. It was remodeled as the "Black Hawk" and sold for use during the Civil War on the Tennessee and Cumberland rivers. Iowa volunteers, seeing it steaming on those waters, were made to feel a little nearer home.

Several other boats navigated the Cedar (1863 to 1884) but steamboating on the Cedar ultimately failed financially. The efforts did help establish Cedar Rapids as a shopping center; movement of freight on the river made lower prices possible. A survey of the river in 1909 concluded that travel was not feasible without large expenditures to make the 248-mile river navigable (Danek, pp. 23, 25). The Cedar empties into the Iowa River in Louisa county some 25 miles from the Mississippi.

Isaac's wife, Sarah

WHEN Isaac's mother inherited money from her family in the 1850s, Mary and Andrew invested in farmland. Isaac would marry on 24 April 1861 before he was 29, acquire his own homestead 12 January 1862, and improve his 40 acres while working on his parents' farm. Both farms were in the Robins area, northwest of Marion; Robins would be established in the late 1880s and named for the family who had owned the land since 1842. Isaac's bride is Miss Sarah Flack, daughter of John and Catherine (Pogue) Flack of Ireland.

Households were established in the county also for Isaac's half-sisters: Mary and Christeen wed in 1842 and 1843, Mary to Edwin Hayes and Christeen to Nathaniel McBride. His brother Michael wed Mary Etta Robinette in 1856. Isaac's younger sisters also married: Amy to James Cronk in 1859, Charlotte to Samuel Mentzer in 1860, and Matilda to Frank Whisler in 1862. Isaac's niece, Christina (daughter of Barnet and Ann Lutz) married in 1860 Henry G. Strong, son of Luman Strong.

Kenwood, where Isaac's sister Ann and husband were living still on their farm, would be platted and named by Mr. Isaac W. Carroll. In 1883 he bought a tract of land "on the

Boulevard near the crossing of the street railway and the Mil-waukee road." Carroll would build a home, and plat 17 other lots. A small town slowly developed and the first store opened in 1884. Incorporation papers for Kenwood were filed in October 1886 and Barnet Lutz became its first mayor.

AFTER we moved to Robins in about 1854, my brother and I made frequent visits to Kenwood. We usually went on foot, walking south from Blairs Ferry Road through a continuous hazel patch. On one of these trips we discovered a wagon track that entered the more beaten road. Starting at Kenwood, we followed that track to see where it came out. We found it aimed in a straight line for the Bowman Springs west of Marion. The track approached the Blairs Ferry Road where big timber with little underbrush began, then scattered and became quite indistinct. A little way to the north the tracks came together again, passing near the Springs where the tracks again scattered. They crossed Dry Creek, circled south of the Bowman farm, then down in a southeasterly direction across swampy grassland to Sulfur Springs before crossing Indian Creek.

Reading between the lines, I surmise the following. First, it was well known that a house had been built in what became Cedar Rapids before Marion had any houses. It was called the Shepard cabin, and used for hiding stolen goods. This house does not seem to be claimed by the early citizens as belonging to the city. Second, two houses had been built outside Marion before any were built in the city. One of these houses, near the Springs, was the home of the Old Bogus Coon *Joel Leverich.* The other, a little farther west, was occupied by a well-known chief of horse thieves *(John Broady).*

The notorious Broady (Brodie) gang from Ohio had drifted into Linn County early in 1839. They came by way of Indiana and Illinois, having made themselves un-welcome in those states. It was known that the Goudy robbers had associated with the Broady gang. The 1840 census lists three Broady households: Stephen Broady with four children, and a man in his fifties; perhaps John the father was living with them. John Jr. and Hugh had no children but each headed a household. All the Broady sons were in their twenties, with William perhaps making his home with John Jr. The Broadys soon moved on again. William "Bill" Broady was arrested later for horse stealing in Fayette county, according to the Marion Register (July 1857). *He escaped while in custody of a county officer, displaying "an ingenuity of conception and energy worthy of better causes." Bill Broady was later seen in Saint Joseph, Missouri* (1878 History, p. 483).

Benjamin Bowman bought "the Broady place" in 1860 after working as a miller for 10 years. Bowman's daughter, Nettie, in 1895 married the youngest son of Henry and Christina Strong. By 1909 "the Broady place" had become the George A. Strong farm. Walter B. Strong was born there in 1901, and brought his bride (Thelma Oliver of Cedar Rapids) there in 1922. Walter and Thelma Strong became the parents of the editor and four other children who survived. All were born in the old Bowman home where their father had made his first appearance.

It is not to be doubted that these two men, *Joel Leverich and John Broady*, had many occasions to visit the Shepard house. It is quite supposable that they made a road of their own from near the Springs to the Shepard cabin. The track I found in the hazel patch would have made a straight route between the two locations. The continuing route from Bowman Springs to Marion, by way of Sulfur Springs, would have been a convenient secret path. It offered greater opportunity for concealment than the regular roadway. Few persons except thieves and robbers made it a place of regular travel.

Marion's celebrated spring water (from 1886 to 1952) evoked much interest. In 1901 a federal government agency proclaimed Marion the "healthiest city in the United States."

A news release had prompted *The Chicago Sunday Tribune* to investigate. *The article, published 13 October 1901, said that Ponce de León, who searched Florida in vain for the "fountain of youth" in 1513 had looked in the wrong place. He should have traveled northwestward, crossed the Mississippi, and gone to Marion, Iowa to realize his dream.* The government agency had calculated the death rate for communities with populations of 1,000 and more. There were nearly twelve hundred such U. S. cities and towns. It found the average death rate to be 17.47 per thousand while Marion (population 5,000) had only seven deaths, a mere 1.4 deaths per thousand. The Tribune reporter discovered that Marion had three fountains. "They are the three springs that provide Marion with the coldest and most sparkling water." A 1927 geologist report tells us more

> The three springs are known as Bowman, Middle, and Lower. All are enclosed in reservoirs, built upon the bedrock. The spring houses have roofs, and openings are screened . . . The flow of these springs has been estimated at 3 million gallons per day. Only 400,000 gallons are used by the City of Marion.

The Tribune story named "Uncle Dickie" Thomas as one of many long-lived citizens. It incorrectly stated that he had lived to 127; he was only 110 when he died in 1892. At the age of 83 he had given up his life of "single wretchedness" to marry a woman 50 years younger than himself. They had a daughter, Mary, who married Dr. Bell English, and gave Thomas a grandson. The facts seem remarkable enough without exaggerating Uncle Dickie's longevity.

Thomas Park Was Named for This Man

Richard "Uncle Dickie" Thomas was 102 when this photo was taken with his two-year-old grandson, Thomas English. Born in Maryland in 1782, he died in Marion, Iowa in 1892 at age 110. When Thomas Park was organized in 1921, I. N. Kramer and Son donated trees and shrubs for landscaping it.

29 Isaac Creating a Career

Merchant Addison Daniels

FEW people know that the first greenhouse in Linn County was built five miles northwest of Marion, seven miles north of Cedar Rapids. It was located near the bottom of the south slope of Wickiup Hill. The name indicates it had been a camping place for Indians. In 1919 the sand hill on the west side of Dry Creek adjoins the city of Robins. I built the greenhouse in 1863. It did not belong to the earliest settlement, nor was it a pretentious building. I constructed the walls by setting up large posts and sided both sides. Then I filled between the siding with sawdust. I used cheap butternut lumber for the rafters and covered them with two dollars worth of imperfect panes of broken glass obtained from Mr. Addison Daniels, a Marion merchant. For cutting the glass, I bought a glass-cutter's diamond for two dollars. This greenhouse was 24 feet long and 12 feet wide with a lean-to roof.

I placed a brick furnace and chimney in the corner; the furnace would take wood four-feet long. A brick flue ran the entire length and across one end to the chimney. The door, made of heavy sheet iron, fit flat against the brick wall of the furnace. The completed door with hangings cost one dollar. Total cash cost of the greenhouse was about ten dollars. *Isaac had seen only one greenhouse; it was a lean-to variety built by a physician who grew medicinal plants and herbs.*

Greenhouses heated by flues and with wood as fuel

did not require night firing. At nine o'clock we could fire up the furnace, close the draft, and sleep until morning. At 30 below zero it might be necessary to add fuel around midnight. There were disadvantages to this heating system. Excessive heat cracked the furnace and flues, causing them to smoke. Frequent repair and soot removal were required, and one fire heated a relatively small space. I built a second greenhouse 12 feet wide and 40 feet long with a span roof. I again bought broken glass from Mr. Daniels. He had been piling it up for more than 20 years, not knowing whether he would ever find any use for the glass.

Many customers from Marion and Cedar Rapids called at my greenhouses. They probably came for an outing as well as to get plants. I also kept plants on sale in both Marion and Cedar Rapids. When I built those houses at Robins, it was not my intention to remain at that location. I had planned to move to Cedar Rapids or Marion as soon as circumstances permitted. Both houses worked satisfactorily until 1867. In that year a big hail storm broke them up, and hastened a move before I was ready. From 800 feet of glass, I saved only 150 feet. It was enough to cover half of a first replacement house. I had 40 acres that I could not sell then. Several years later I sold the land for a thousand dollars, but had to wait for part of the payment. I found a desirable five acres in Cedar Rapids, but could not force myself to venture on it. In 1867 I secured my present *(1919)* location in Marion. It did not require any down payment on my part. The site was covered with stumps, and there was no house on it. I had no money to build one, and a family to support. The lumber man and merchants of Marion, by generous credit, helped me through.

Isaac did not mention the county's first bank that had been "founded in 1863 by some of the leading citizens of Marion." Redman D. Stephens was its president. The bank was named the First National, and was Iowa's first national bank. Stephens later founded the Merchants National Bank in Cedar Rapids. Both banks in the late 1900s became part of larger banks. First National was taken over by Norwest, and MNB by Firstar. Many pioneer settlers distrusted banks during the Civil War.

By myself I built a little 14 by 18 feet house, and a greenhouse 12 x 18 feet south of the house. I covered the lower half with six sashes saved from the hail wreck, and the upper half with lumber. Sunlight shone to the back through glass on the front, enabling me to produce quite a stock of plants. I started hot beds, and gardened among the stumps as best I could. I sold vegetable and sweet potato plants, and was able to meet all of my contracts and pay some on my land.

Isaac Kramer's advertisement appeared in the Marion Register of 13 March 1867. He offered "100,000 sweet-potato plants for sale." Delivery would be made at the home of John Magee (Oxley Vol. II, p. 32). *Magee, a half-brother of Isaac's wife, came to Marion in 1861.*

Then I began building more greenhouses as did others. One was two miles east of Robins, one two miles north of Marion, and three were in Cedar Rapids on the southeast side of Second Avenue between Sixth and Ninth streets. All greenhouses were patterned after those put up by Mr. Henderson, New York's most notable gardener and florist. They measured 12 feet wide. After trying small houses of different styles, I ventured on a house 28 feet wide and 70 feet long with three flues. It developed that I did not need the middle flue because the heat followed up inside the glass to the comb, not allowing the middle of the house to get cold. This house worked so well that I later built another like it. When steam heating came into vogue, narrow houses were abandoned everywhere.

Isaac had opened a warehouse and sales room in Cedar Rapids by 1885; it was a few years after electricity first came to the city. Moreover, he had built a nicer, larger home for his family north of the greenhouse. He continued to supervise the operation in Marion. His son Judson, now in his early twenties, was in charge at the retail store in downtown Cedar Rapids. The business continued for more than 50 years.

I. N. KRAMER & SON.

Seedsmen and Florists, Nos. 225 and 227 Third Ave., Cedar Rapids, Iowa.—One of the most extensive establishments of its kind in the state is that of I. N. Kramer & Son, wholesale and retail dealers in seeds, plants, bulbs, cut flowers, etc., with warehouse and salesroom at Nos. 235 and 227 Third avenue, and greenhouse located at Marion. As a matter of fact, this is the oldest and most prominent enterprise of the kind in Central Iowa. The business was established thirty years ago in Marion, and at Cedar Rapids the firm has been located for the past 15 years. The greenhouses, which are under the personal supervision of Mr. I. N. Kramer, an experienced and practical florist, embrace fully 15,000 square feet of glass, and several acres of ground. At the greenhouses and grounds of the firm may be found one of the most complete and the largest assortment of plants and flowers in Iowa, which have been selected with discriminating taste and developed to the highest degree of perfection. Mr. J. A. Kramer, who has practically grown up in the business, has charge of the house in this city. The stock carried here is large, choice and comprehensive, including field, grass and garden seeds, embracing timothy and clover seeds, lawn grass seeds, flower seeds, etc. Seeds are grown expressly for this house by the most expert and careful seed growers of the United States and Europe. The business of this representative and reliable firm extends all over the United States and is increasing in volume and importance each year. The firm issues an illustrated catalogue containing useful information pertaining to cut flowers, farm and garden seeds; flower seeds, flowering and ornamental plants, etc., which may be had free upon application.

The firm flourished until 1920 when Isaac's son, Judson (above), died of a heart attack while cranking the delivery truck. In 1921 Isaac sold the nursery business to a firm in Ottumwa; Bezdek's acquired the property late in the thirties.

Clipping is from the 1900 Cedar Rapids *Illustrated Review* (Courtesy Cedar Rapids Public Library)

The Kramer home in 1914 . . .

Isaac's Victorian home (above), north side of The Boulevard. Isaac (center); his children stand right: Adelaide, Judson, and Ella Lund. Beside are his sisters Charlotte (left) and Amy. At left: Einer Lund, grandson; Samuel Mentzer, brother-in-law.

... and greenhouses in Marion

Judson Kramer and his father, Isaac, (foreground right) stand before the greenhouses. Their home is visible right of windmill.

ISAAC'S BROTHER

Michael N. Kramer
Born 26 April 1830,
Pennsylvania;
married 1856, Iowa;
four children;
died 25 August 1917,
California

Old Settlers Pose on Courthouse Steps, 1891

Thirty-six "Old Settlers of 1839" posed on the courthouse steps at Marion in 1891. Of 20 shown here seven are members of the Kramer family—two in the back row, five in the middle row. Photo was cropped to enlarge their images. History books record that Mrs. Brown, front row, arrived in Linn County in 1854; her husband Horace was the son of early settler, Nathan Brown.

Back row: Barnet and Ann Lutz are right of center. Left are Mrs. Torrance, Mrs. Railsback, unidentified man; the Lutzs, unidentified man, and George Cone.

Middle: Lewis Kramer, brother; unidentified woman; Andrew Kramer, father; William A. Kramer, nephew; Isaac Kramer, Charlotte and Sam Mentzer, Amy Cronk, sisters and brother-in-law.

Front: Dorcas Beall, Elihu Ives, Horace and Mrs. Brown, George Yeisley.

30   Changes in the 1900s

AFTER a sixty-year absence from Linn Grove, I returned for a visit in 1917. What I found was a surprise. Stopping to water my horse, I asked the lady of the house the distance to the Grove. She said I had passed it a mile back. I insisted that the Grove was still ahead of me. It developed that she spoke of the Presbyterian church. It was the only Linn Grove she knew. She did not know that I was referring to what once had been timberland. The Grove itself no longer retains its identity. For nearly eighty years the 7,000 acres had been honeycombed—the best of its timber and much of its lumber timber had been cut. Young growth had been cleared to make farmland; but the land we had occupied had more than a hundred acres of timber, and had extended westward.

I had wandered Linn Grove for twelve years in my youth, and was familiar with it all. I knew the beautiful flowers in the timber and on the prairie, and the towering trees. *Isaac listed herbs and flowers he had seen in the early Grove: clumps of large pink moccasin or lady slipper, quantities of ginseng, spikenard, and sarsaparilla, violets, anemone, bluebells, wood phlox, "aster in the woods," eupatoriums, bloodroot, Bertha root, claytonia, Dutchman's-breeches, cardinal flowers (red lobelia).*

He described what he was seeing in his mind's eye. Seen from a distance, the most attractive plant of the prairie was the fireball with its bright red terminal bract. Prairie phlox growing about 15 inches high in large compact patches had multi-colored flowers. The large succulent leaves and pink flowers of prairie oxalis, or sorrel, was used for making pies of excellent flavor; water bags connected with its roots resembled the icicle radish. A cut-leafed variety of violets grew on the prairie. There were many varieties of yellow flowers (of the black-eyed Susan order). A large variety of asters, blue and purple, also flourished. Nearly all of these have perished with the Grove—along with the prairie grasses.

From a distance I noticed little difference between the Grove and the surrounding land. Up close one can discern that the replanted patches of timber were not so tall nor so free from limbs as the original grove timber. Also the trees were of different varieties. The stately ones, noble oaks, beautiful ash, grand old maples, were all gone. The great trees that I knew and adored will be seen no longer. Gone are the spreading-branched elms, six feet across the stump. Gone is the magnificent linden trunk, four feet in diameter and stretching fifty feet into the sky without a limb.

As Isaac noted during his 25-mile horseback ride, the native beauty of departed groves can never be restored. Groves and farmlands were made to disappear, but satellite communities and the metropolis named Cedar Rapids emerged. It became not only the county seat with the new courthouse on the island; it developed as eastern Iowa's premier city—just as Judge Greene had envisioned it. We could call George Greene "the father of Cedar Rapids" for helping bring it about.

Downtown Cedar Rapids in the early 1900s

Afterword

by Jean Strong

At age 85 Isaac threshed wheat with a flail

WHEN ISAAC KRAMER ENDED WORK ON HIS book manuscript in 1919, he was sharing the family home on Marion Boulevard with son Judson and daughter Adelaide. His wife, Sarah, had died in 1915. Judson died in 1920. It is not surprising that a year later I. N. Kramer & Son donated a quantity of trees and shrubs for landscaping the new park that was established nearby, and named for the original land owner—Richard Thomas. Isaac then sold his business property and moved to his retirement home at 501 Ninth avenue, near the Church of God in Marion where he had occupied the pulpit from 1888 until 1896.

In 1917 Isaac had planted and raised a good crop of wheat. Mindful of earlier days, he harvested part of it with a cradle scythe, and threshed it with a flail. A news story said that on his 86th birthday he was eating bread baked with flour "he had ground with a small hand mill." The writer added, "He ought to have a medal for his industry and loyalty to his country." The First World War was raging in Europe.

Isaac himself outlived most of his family. A daughter and a son had died in infancy (ages 2 and 5) in 1868 and 1878. His father, Andrew, had died at 81 in 1872 and his mother in 1877. His sister Mary Hayes died in 1895, brother Lewis in 1896, sister Christeen McBride in 1898, brother Andrew in 1899, nephew

125

William A. in 1916, brother Michael in 1917 at 87.

Ten weeks before his ninety-first birthday Isaac died at home (23 February 1923) following a brief illness. His obituary recalled his birth at New Geneva, Pennsylvania, on 19 May 1832, his arrival in Iowa in 1839, his lifetime of achievements. Although Isaac did not mention it in his manuscript, his obituary reveals that he had spent less than one year of his adult life outside Linn County—while "attending school in New York at Madison University."

Two daughters, Adelaide at home and Ella Lund of Alexandria, Virginia, survived Isaac as did two grandsons, Einer and Harry Lund. Isaac's three younger sisters (Amy, Charlotte, and Matilda) and numerous nieces and nephews also lived on. His great-niece Clara Viola "Ola" Cronk (1897-1972) gained fame as movie actress "Claire Windsor" in silent movies of the twenties.

My sister, Eileen Strong Minor, was born the year before Isaac died. I entered the Iowa farm scene two years after Isaac's death, and first learned about him sixty-one years later when I discovered his manuscript.

Daughter Adelaide explained the meaning of her father's middle initial in a letter to Benjamin Shambaugh preserved at the State Historical Society in Iowa City

> The "N" does not stand for any name. I remember hearing my father laugh and tell us he was only named Isaac but that he always wished for a middle name or at least an initial. In thinking it over he decided to adopt the letter "N" as that would make his initials spell INK. He always signed his name I. N. or Isaac N. Kramer.

In 1927 Adelaide married a widower in Marion; the people of Kenwood voted their village into the city of Cedar Rapids. Since the late 1930s the Kramer & Son nursery site has been occupied by Bezdek florists. Although U.S. Highway 30 has long since been rerouted to the southern edge of Cedar Rapids, Thomas Park is still popular. Blairs Ferry Road, which Isaac saw as a road to nowhere, is a major access road to Intrastate 380 that carries travelers around city traffic, gains entry to different parts of the Cedar

Rapids metropolitan area, or reaches Iowa City to the south and Waterloo to the north—all in record time.

In 1939 Cedar Rapids businessman Adolf Boyson, a jeweler, bought the Strong farm. It was sold to settle the George A. Strong estate. Walter Strong moved his family to Linn Grove in 1940 and then as his health failed, to Kenwood in Cedar Rapids. My father coincidentally was following his ancestors' footsteps.

When Roy Skogman began a housing development west of the Broady-Bowman-Strong-Boyson farmland in the 1960s, he named it Bowman Woods with the blessing of another Bowman descendant (Wilbur Sebern). Late in the twentieth century interstate highways crisscross the country, as passenger railroads had done in Isaac's time. Regular church services are conducted still at the Presbyterian church in Linn Grove, where friends and members observed its 150th anniversary in 1991. Isaac's older grandson, Einer Lund, survived the Battle of the Bulge in the Second World War to work at the Pentagon, and in 1950 to marry. He and his bride died in an auto accident during their honeymoon.

The younger grandson, Harry V. Lund, and his wife had two sons; one of them produced two girls and three boys; the other, three girls. Seven of these great-great-grandchildren were living in 1996, as were their nine children, whose ages range from one to 14. The seven families were living in New York, Hawaii, Florida, and Washington, D.C.

Only one percent of Iowa's original prairie grasses survive, but a prairie restoration is accessible in Cedar county. The National Park Service in 1971 replaced 76 acres of corn and soy beans with prairie grasses. The restoration is near the Herbert Hoover birthplace, presidential library and museum, and graves of the former President and First Lady (Mrs. Lou Henry Hoover). The site is just north of Interstate 80 at the West Branch exit.

As you gaze over the restored prairie, remember Isaac and his devotion to living and writing the record he left for us.

A: Isaac's Ancestors

Isaac wrote briefly about his family roots. His grandfather, Baltzer Kramer, immigrated to America from Alsace-Lorraine in 1773, motivated by a desire to escape an unpopular king's war. His grandmother, also of German descent, gained passage across the ocean as an indentured servant. The ship's captain paid her passage, and sold her remaining service to another party in America. Such servitude was common and typically lasted four or five years. Baltzer Kramer met Margaretta (Volsin or Repert?), paid off her debt, and married her in 1775.

The immigrant Kramers lived in Frederick county, Maryland, where Baltzer was one of America's pioneer glass blowers. He worked at Pipe Creek in Maryland, and later in Greensboro, Pennsylvania, at the glass factory owned by Swiss-born Albert Gallatin. (Gallatin served as secretary of treasury under President Thomas Jefferson.) Andrew Kramer, born in 1790, learned glass blowing when he was 16.

Kramer glass, known for its brilliant green color, was typical of products from the New Geneva and Greensboro glass works. Examples of Kramer glass are displayed in a glass museum at Waynesburg College, Waynesburg, Pennsylvania.

Baltzer's heirs are named in his will, preserved in a will book (Vol. 1, p. 330, Springhill township, Fayette county, Pennsylvania). He died in 1813; the will was probated 8 February 1814. His heirs were wife Margaret, youngest son **Andrew Kramer**, daughter and son-in-law Polly and Jeremiah Axton, daughters Margaret Reitz and Christina Scott, and sons Baltzer II and George Kramer.

B: Family Lineage Charts

KRAMER LINEAGE

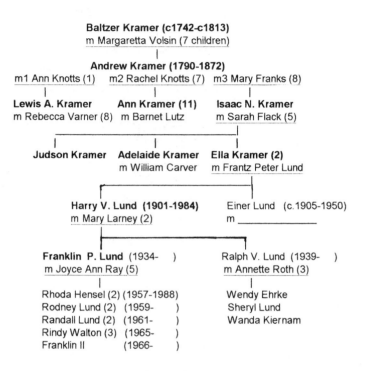

Baltzer Kramer (c1742-c1813)
m Margaretta Volsin (7 children)
|
Andrew Kramer (1790-1872)
m1 Ann Knotts (1)   m2 Rachel Knotts (7)   m3 Mary Franks (8)
| | |
Lewis A. Kramer   **Ann Kramer (11)**   **Isaac N. Kramer**
m Rebecca Varner (8) m Barnet Lutz   m Sarah Flack (5)

Judson Kramer   **Adelaide Kramer**   **Ella Kramer (2)**
                    m William Carver   m Frantz Peter Lund

Harry V. Lund (1901-1984)   Einer Lund   (c.1905-1950)
m Mary Larney (2)   m _____

Franklin P. Lund (1934-)   Ralph V. Lund (1939-)
m Joyce Ann Ray (5)   m Annette Roth (3)
| |
Rhoda Hensel (2) (1957-1988)   Wendy Ehrke
Rodney Lund (2) (1959-   )   Sheryl Lund
Randall Lund (2) (1961-   )   Wanda Kiernam
Rindy Walton (3) (1965-   )
Franklin II   (1966-   )

LUTZ LINEAGE

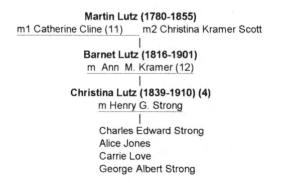

Martin Lutz (1780-1855)
m1 Catherine Cline (11)   m2 Christina Kramer Scott
|
Barnet Lutz (1816-1901)
m Ann M. Kramer (12)
|
Christina Lutz (1839-1910) (4)
m Henry G. Strong
|
Charles Edward Strong
Alice Jones
Carrie Love
George Albert Strong

BOWMAN LINEAGE
(Buman, Bauman, Bowman)

Wendel Bauman (1681-1735)
m Anne _____
|
Benjamin Bowman (ca 1712-1775/80)
m Anna _____
|
Joseph Bowman (1745/50-1811)
m Faronica Buckwalter
|
Joseph Bowman II (1777-1831)
m Ann Bowman
|
Daniel Bowman (1804-1870)
m Mary Smith (8)
|
Benjamin Bowman II (1830-1902)
m Eliza Wilson (6)
|
Nettie L. Bowman (1869-1914) (2)
m George A. Strong
|
Dale Bowman Strong
Walter Benjamin Strong

STRONG LINEAGE

Luman Mastin Strong   **(1803-1867)**
m1 Nancy Griswold (7)   m2 Mary Gabbert (3)
| |
Henry G. Strong (1834-1915)   Orville Strong (1843-1931)
m Christina Lutz (4)   m1 Louise Sims (3)
| m2 Minnie Carkeek (5)
George A. Strong (1870-1936)
m1 Nettie L. Bowman (2)   m2 Ida M. Crowley
|
Walter B. Strong (1901-1951)
m Thelma I. Oliver (5)
|
Eileen E. Minor (4)
    m Maurice C. Minor
Jean Strong
    (single blessed)
George W. Strong (1928-1994)
    m Darlene E. Moser (2) (1929-1989)
Doris M. Neal (4)
    m Norman L. Neal
Ruth A. Armstrong (1)
    m John V. Armstrong

John Oliver (c1699-1741)
m Margaret
|
George Oliver (1726/7-1786)
m1 Jemima Reagan (9)   m Martha Whitworth (3)
|
James Oliver (c1756-1840)
m Susannah Lemons (8)
|
Samuel Oliver (1794-1843)
m Ruth Obedience Alley (13)
|
John Hiram Oliver (1831-1920)
m Elizabeth "Eliza" Drennan (11)
|
Samuel Ellsworth Oliver (1858-1931)
m Mary Elizabeth Morgan (11)
|
Thelma Iris Oliver (1900-1978)
m Walter B. Strong (5)

C: Postscript

The Strong, Kramer and Lutz families set foot in eastern Iowa as early as 1837, 1838, and 1839. The Bowmans came in 1856; the Olivers in 1914.

The Oliver family of Scotch Irish descent arrived in the Jerseys in the early 1700s, then moved to Virginia. Their son George Oliver, born in Albemarle county, Virginia, established his large family in Rockingham county along the Dan river in North Carolina. He and four of his 10 sons fought in the Revolutionary battle at the Guilford County Courthouse (Oliver, p. 280). Obedience Alley Oliver, widow of Samuel I, moved her family in 1845 to Jefferson county, Indiana (Oliver, p. 285). Thelma I. Oliver, daughter of Samuel II, joined her parents in Cedar Rapids in 1915, and did not return with them when they went back to Indiana in 1919. She was employed as bookkeeper at the Kaiser Shoe Store.

The Bowmans (then Bumans) have been traced to Zurich, Switzerland in 1369 (by Wilbur Sebern). Wendel Bowman (then Bauman), a coppersmith, came to America in 1707 and settled in Lancaster county, Pennsylvania. Benjamin Bowman II, a miller, moved to Ohio in 1850, and to Linn county, Iowa in 1856.

Luman M. Strong, born in Vermont, later lived in Ohio where his first wife died in 1835. He moved to Iowa. His second wife had been a school teacher in Davenport. They lived in Linn county 1839-1847, and died in Dodgeville, Wisconsin. Three of Luman's sons and a daughter from his first marriage settled in Iowa eventually. Daughter Emily married Charles C. Cook and they lived in Cedar Rapids. Son Henry G. Strong married Christina Lutz in 1860.

References

Arnold, Onalee. Genealogist-historian. 1987 interview with Jean Strong.

Atlas of Linn County, Iowa. 1907. Davenport: The Iowa Publishing Co.

Baker, Brigadier General Nathaniel B. 1867. *Report to the Governor of Iowa, Vol. II.*

Boatner, Mark Mayo III. 1959. *The Civil War Dictionary.* New York: David McKay Co.

Brewer, Luther A. and Barthinius L. Wick. 1911. *History of Linn County Iowa.* Vol. I and II. Chicago: Pioneer Publishing Co.

Brown, Don Doyle. 1965. *Tell a Tale of Iowa.* Des Moines: Wallace-Homestead Co.

Carroll, Rev. George R. 1895. *Pioneer Life In and Around Cedar Rapids, Iowa.* Cedar Rapids: Times Printing and Binding House.

Chapman Bros. 1887. *Portrait and Biographical Album of Linn County.* Chicago: Chapman Brothers.

Christensen, Thomas P. 1954. *Indians, A Brief History.* Cedar Rapids: Laurance Press.

Clarke, S. J. 1901. *Biographical Record of Linn County.* Chicago: S. J. Clarke Publishing Co.

Danek, Ernie. 1980. *Tall Corn and High Technology: Cedar Rapids A Pictorial History.* Woodland Hills, Calif.: Windsor Publications.

Durham, Samuel W., papers at State Historical Society, Iowa City, Iowa.

Dwelle, Jessie Merrill. 1954. Revised by Ruth H. Wagner. *Iowa Beautiful Land, A History of Iowa.* Mason City: Klipto Loose Leaf Co.

Ellis, Franklin, editor. 1882. *History of Fayette County, Pennsylvania.* Vol. II. Philadelphia: L. H. Everts & Co.

Gest, Neil C. and Parke G. Smith. March 1939. "The Glassmaking Kramers." *Antiques* magazine.

Hastie, Eugene N. 1966. *High Points of Iowa History.* N.p.

Hills, Leon C. 1938. *History and Legends of Place Names in Iowa, the Meaning of Our Map.* Omaha: Omaha School Supply.

History of Linn County. 1878. Chicago: Western Historical Co.

Houlette, William. 1970. *Iowa, the Pioneer Heritage.* Des Moines: Wallace-Homestead Book Co.

Jack, O. G. 1870. *A Brief History of Muscatine.* Muscatine: Journal Book and Job Publishing House.

Johnson, Mrs. Russell and Mrs. Donald Koppenhaver. Typescript 1966. "History of Linn Grove Presbyterian Church 1841-1966."

Kirkpatrick, Inez E. Typescript 1975. "Stagecoach Trails in Iowa." Crete, Nebraska: J-B Publishing Co.

Koppenhaver, Bertha, and others. 1981. *Springville, Iowa 1881-1981.*

Kramer Family Genealogical Records. Courtesy of Nelda Y. Miller (Mrs. Charles) Hoover, Cedar Rapids.

Laws of the Territory of Iowa, 1838-1839.

Lazell, Fred J. 1923. *Linn County: A Brief Review of Its History from 1838 to 1923.* Linn County: Board of Supervisors.

Lettermann, Edward J. 1972. *Pioneer Farming in Iowa.* Des Moines: Living History Farms.

Lloyd, James T. 1856. *Lloyd's Steamboat Directory and Disasters on the Western Waters.* Cincinnati: James T. Lloyd and Co.

Map of Linn County, Iowa. 1859. Chicago: McWilliams & Thompson. Courtesy of Marvin Oxley. Distributed by Linn County Heritage Society.

Map of Linn County, Iowa. 1869. Geneva, Ill.: Thompson and Everts. Distributed by Linn County Heritage Society.

Maxfield, Marie M., and others. 1988. *Robins, Iowa Centennial.*

McKean, Thomas J. Civil War pensions file. National Archives, Washington, DC. Invalid pension file No. 155998; widow's pension file No. 187647.

Mott, D. C. 1930-1932. *Abandoned Towns, Villages, and Post Offices of Iowa.* Reprinted from Annals of Iowa, Vols. XVII and XVIII.

Murray, Janette Stevenson and Frederick Gray Murray. 1950. *The Story of Cedar Rapids.* NY: Stratford House.

Norwood, Frederick A. 1974. *The Story of American Methodism.* Nashville, Tenn.: Abington Press. Courtesy of Joyce Parks, historian, Marion Methodist Church.

Orchard, Hugh A. 1923. *Fifty Years of Chautauqua.* Cedar Rapids: The Torch Press.

Oxley, Marvin. Typescript ca 1946. *History of Marion.* Four volumes. Bound, Marion Public Library.

Oxley, Marvin. Unpublished typescript ca 1950. "Old Water Mills of Linn County." Courtesy of Mike and Jean Oxley.

Reid, Harvey. 1909. Edited by Benjamin F. Shambaugh. *Thomas Cox.* Iowa City: State Historical Society of Iowa.

Ross, Earl D. 1951. *Iowa Agriculture: An Historical Survey.* Iowa City: State Historical Society of Iowa.

Schwieder, Dorothy and Thomas J. Morain, and Lynn Nielsen. 1989, 1991. *Iowa Past to Present, The People and the Prairie.* Ames: Iowa State University Press.

Smithsonian Book of Invention. 1978. Washington, DC: Smithsonian Exposition Books.

Strong, Jean 1965. *Herbert Hoover 1874-1964.* Special issue of *Iowa Illustrated* magazine. Cedar Rapids: Jean Strong Publications.

Swisher, Jacob A. 1940. *Iowa—Land of Many Mills.* Iowa City: State Historical Society of Iowa.

INDEX